Information Literacy in the Workplace

Edited by
Marc Forster

facet
publishing

Published by Facet Publishing,
7 Ridgmount Street, London WC1E 7AE
www.facetpublishing.co.uk

Facet Publishing is wholly owned by CILIP:
the Library and Information Association.

British Library Cataloguing in Publication Data
A catalogue record for this book is available from
the British Library.

ISBN 978-1-78330-132-4 (paperback)
ISBN 978-1-78330-133-1 (hardback)
ISBN 978-1-78330-134-8 (e-book)

First published 2017

Text printed on FSC accredited material.

Typeset from editor's files by Flagholme Publishing Services in
10/13 pt Palatino Linotype and Franklin Gothic.
Printed and made in Great Britain by CPI Group (UK) Ltd,
Croydon, CR0 4YY.

Information Literacy in the Workplace

Every purchase of a Facet book helps to fund CILIP's advocacy, awareness and accreditation programmes for information professionals.

Contents

Figures and tables   vii
Contributors   ix
Foreword   xiii
Jane Secker

1 Information Literacy and the workplace: new concepts, new perspectives?   1
Marc Forster

2 How is Information Literacy experienced in the workplace?   11
Marc Forster

3 Information Literacy and the personal dimension: team players, empowered
   clients and career development   29
Marc Forster

4 From transaction to transformation: organizational learning and knowledge
   creation experience within Informed Systems   41
Mary M. Somerville and Christine S. Bruce

5 Virtuality at work: an enabler of professional Information Literacy   57
Elham Sayyad Abdi

6 Determining the value of Information Literacy for employers   67
Stéphane Goldstein and Andrew Whitworth

7 Information Literacy's role in workplace competence, 'best practice' and
   the ethics of professional obligation   85
Marc Forster

8   Learning within for beyond: exploring a workplace Information Literacy design   97
    Annemaree Lloyd

9   Developing information professional competences in disciplinary domains: a
    challenge for higher education   113
    Stephen Roberts

10 The 'hidden' value of Information Literacy in the workplace context: how
    to unlock and create value   131
    Bonnie Cheuk

11 The 'Workplace Experience Framework' and evidence-based Information
    Literacy education   149
    Marc Forster

References   165
Index   181

Figures and tables

Figures

2.1 Relationship between dimensions, themes and Categories of Description 22

5.1 Information Literacy as experienced by web professionals 64

6.1 Value propositions relevant to Information Literacy 72

6.2 The DeVIL tool 81

8.1 DASIL (Dimensions of Activity and Skills of Information Literacy: a practice-based model) 107

8.2 Enactment of Information Literacy practice 108

9.1 The 14-theme PIIK model 121

11.1 Information Literacy questionnaire 163

Tables

11.1 Dimensions of Variation traced in the first interview transcript 159

11.2 Dimensions of Variation traced in the second interview transcript 159

11.3 Categories of Description from the first interview 161

11.4 Categories of Description from the second interview 161

Contributors

Professor Christine S. Bruce is Professor in the Information Systems School at the Queensland University of Technology (QUT), in Brisbane, Australia. She is a Principal Fellow of the UK Higher Education Academy and was an Australian Learning and Teaching Fellow in 2009. She is also Academic Program Director – Research Training for the Science and Engineering Faculty, and Convenor of the QUT Higher Education Research Network. Her research focuses include information literacy and information literacy education, postgraduate study and supervision, and qualitative research methods; with specific attention to informed learning, information and learning experiences and phenomenography. Her current work incorporates a focus on academic, workplace and community environments, especially learning experiences in innovative technological spaces. Her recent books include *Informed Learning*, published by the ALA in 2008 and *Information Experience*, published by Emerald in 2014, co-edited with Kate Davis, Hilary Hughes, Helen Partridge and Ian Stoodley.

Dr Bonnie Cheuk is an executive with the global financial institution Euroclear, with significant practical expertise in digital transformation, digital channel management, information and knowledge management, collaboration, social media and Enterprise 2.0, through 20 years of international working experience with multinational corporations. She blends an interest in change management and communication/facilitation skills, and a passion to understand knowledge workers' and customers' needs, with a deep understanding of the latest technologies to deliver business solutions and drive change. Born in Hong Kong, she has a first degree in Economics from the Chinese University of Hong Kong, and a Master's in Library and Information Science (distinction) from the University of Wales, Aberystwyth.

Under the mentorship of Dr Brenda Dervin, she completed her PhD on how auditors, engineers and architects look for information in the workplace context in Singapore. Her paper 'Information Literacy in the Workplace Context: issues, best practices and challenges' was commissioned by UNESCO, the US National Commission on Libraries and Information Science and the National Forum on Information Literacy, for the 2002 Information Literacy Meeting of Experts, Prague. She is currently partnering with business and technology leaders to establish a vision for Knowledge and Collaboration in the Digital Workplace to improve digital client experience. She is the author of *Social Strategies in Action: driving business transformation*, published by Ark Group in 2013. She is married with one daughter and lives in London.

Dr Marc Forster is a librarian at the University of West London, looking after the needs of the College of Nursing, Midwifery and Healthcare. His research interests include Information Literacy's role in learning and in the performance of the professional role.

Stéphane Goldstein is Executive Director of InformAll, which, through research, analysis and facilitation, promotes the relevance, importance and benefits of Information Literacy (IL) in the library world and beyond. He is the author of reports, articles and other material on the relevance and applicability of IL to a range of settings, particularly in the context of the workplace. He is a strong advocate for IL and, as such, brokers relationships between information professionals and other stakeholders, and facilitates joint projects. He previously spent ten years at the Research Information Network (RIN), where he led on Information Literacy activities; there he was also responsible for project management and policy formulation in the broad area of information as input and output of the research process. He previously worked in a range of science and research policy roles at the Medical Research Council and Research Councils UK.

Professor Annemaree Lloyd has worked in vocational and higher education institutions in Australia since 2002. She is currently a Professor at the Swedish School of Library and Information Science, University of Borås, Sweden, where she leads the information practice research group. Her research explores the interconnection between people, information and practice. Her research programme has two strands. The first focuses on concepts of practice and landscape in the context of workplace information practices, information and digital literacy, embodied learning, and communities of practice. The second strand focuses on the relationships between information practice, information resilience and social inclusion. She has been recognized for her research and scholarship through the receipt of a European Commission

Erasmus Mundus Scholarship and Research Excellence Awards. She has been a Research Fellow at RIPPLE (Research Institute for Professional Practice, Learning and Education) at Charles Sturt University. She has published extensively in the area of Information Literacy.

Dr Stephen Roberts began a research career in social sciences information systems (at the University of Bath) and library management (at Cambridge and Loughborough universities) following a degree in Geography at the University of Cambridge and a postgraduate degree at the University of Sheffield. He was awarded a PhD in 1983 from Loughborough University for work on social science information. He has been associated since 1983 with information professional education at the University of West London, where he is currently Associate Professor (Information Management). He has published extensively in the library and information field on social science information, financial and resource management, information policy and professional issues and theory. He has contributed to professional bodies such as IFLA and CILIP, and, amongst other international professional activities, has taught in China, Cuba and Mexico. Although retired since 2016, he is still active in doctoral supervision, and in researching and writing in knowledge management, information and education, and information development in different settings. Continuing research interests include scientific information and communication, information policy, and strategy and applications in various organizational settings, such as urban planning and project management. He is currently an external examiner in information management at the University of the West of England in Bristol.

Dr Elham Sayyad Abdi is an associate lecturer in the Information Systems School, Queensland University of Technology (QUT). She is a member of QUT's Information Studies Group, a research team with a focus on information experiences. Her research interests are in Information Literacy and how it can be developed, specifically within an everyday life context. Her recent research activities have focused on immigrants' information experience and the concept of information experience design as an enabler of Information Literacy. She is currently leading a three-year Australian Research Council-funded project on migrants' Information Literacy. In 2017, she will also co-lead a project to investigate how libraries can enhance the information experience of non-library user refugees. She has a library and information science background and has been an active member of the library and information profession. She is a committee member of the Australian Library and Information Association, Queensland and, at an international level, the secretary for the Association for Information Science and Technology (ASIS&T), Asia–Pacific Chapter. She has also served on the organizing and programme committee of local and international conferences and symposiums.

Professor Mary M. Somerville serves as University Librarian for University of the Pacific Libraries in Sacramento, San Francisco, and Stockton, California, USA. Her leadership approach combines participatory design and Informed Learning to create conditions for workplace learning. An Informed Systems approach enables information-sharing processes and knowledge creation activities that foster information exchange and knowledge creation through co-designed communication systems, information practices and Informed Learning. Antecedent theory and best practices for Informed Systems' leadership essentials and collaboration processes are presented in *Informed Systems: organizational design for learning in action*, published in 2015 by Chandos Press, a subsidiary of Elsevier. She also serves as Adjunct Professor in the School of Information Systems, in the Science and Engineering Faculty, at Queensland University of Technology, in Brisbane, Australia. In 2010, she received the Distinguished Scholar Award from the School of Information (iSchool) at San José State University, California, USA.

Dr Andrew Whitworth is Director of Teaching and Learning Strategy at the Manchester Institute of Education, University of Manchester, UK. He has published two single-authored books on Digital and Information Literacy: *Information Obesity* (2009) and *Radical Information Literacy* (2014). He was one of the authors of the 2012 Moscow Declaration on Media and Information Literacy and in 2017 will be keynote speaker at the European Conference on Information Literacy.

Foreword

I was delighted to be asked to write the Foreword to this book, which bridges an important gap between the Information Literacy work researchers and practitioners do in higher education, with the support that is needed in the workplace. Better collaboration between information professionals in all sectors has long been aspired to, but it is only relatively recently that work is being done to join the dots between Information Literacy initiatives in schools, higher education and the workplace. Understanding how people's 'information landscapes' (Lloyd, 2010) shift as they transition to a new environment is hugely relevant and this book offers us new perspectives.

I was particularly pleased to be invited to write this Foreword, as I am indebted to Marc Forster for a number of reasons. Most recently he has been a valuable addition to the CILIP Information Literacy Group's committee. And it was through his doctoral work that I first properly engaged with the research methodology, phenomenography, a methodology that originated in the field of education but has been used increasingly in Information Literacy research (Yates, Partridge and Bruce, 2012) in recent years. A qualitative methodology, it is concerned with the variation in the way phenomena are 'experienced'. Understanding of the variations in the way Information Literacy is experienced and so given 'meaning', often in terms of the personal or collaborative knowledge it develops, helps us see how Information Literacy contributes to work, study and other aspects of our daily lives. I was already familiar with the work of Christine S. Bruce and the seven faces of Information Literacy; however, through Marc's work I saw how looking at themes and variations of complexity within experiences of Information Literacy translated into the work that I did on a day-to-day basis. Interacting with another person's work is an enlightening, highly reflective and iterative process and one that can fundamentally change our understanding of a subject.

I became familiar with Marc's work around the same time that I was compiling a response to the draft Information Literacy framework issued by the Association of College and Research Libraries (ACRL) in the USA, and so as well as reading up on phenomenography I was becoming aware of threshold concepts and the notion of liminality, mainly through the writing of Barbara Fister (Fister, 2015). The notion of passing through a portal is for me a wonderful metaphor for learning. When I've carried out research in the past I often know I am on the verge of a meaningful breakthrough when I am struggling deeply to assimilate some new knowledge with what I think I already know. Phenomenography was for me a threshold concept, but through Marc's work I've passed through that portal and I am fundamentally changed by it. It wasn't easy and I am also grateful to Emma Coonan for her insights and the discussions we had along the way. My experiences of meeting Marc left me wondering how Emma and I might have conceived 'A New Curriculum for Information Literacy' (ANCIL) if we'd used this research method in 2011, when we carried out our research together (Secker and Coonan, 2013). I hope it is perhaps something in future we can return to, when we could have another go at 'Rethinking Information Literacy'! The theme of transitions was very important in ANCIL as we looked at the Information Literacy support students need on entering higher education from school, and on leaving university to enter the workplace. Understanding more about this experience, and more deeply through phenomenography, seems to me to be the next step.

The work presented in this book resonated with me, as I have always believed that Information Literacy is something that matters at least as much when a person leaves formal education and enters the workplace, or needs to deal with information in their day-to-day life. Having spent most of my career working in higher education, supporting academic staff, many of whom are extremely experienced researchers and teachers, I have observed how Information Literacy is an ongoing process that evolves and develops throughout one's career. It's not something we can achieve and check off as complete through taking a one-off course. That said, developing critical evaluation skills while in formal education must surely put you at an advantage on entering the workplace, provided you recognize how your information landscape has shifted. For me Information Literacy is always contextual and that is why it is helpful to customize our Information Literacy interventions in what has been described as the 'boutique model' (Secker, 2012).

Several years later I was inspired to test out phenomenography in a study of librarians' experiences of copyright with my co-researcher and fellow copyright education enthusiast Chris Morrison (Secker and Morrison, 2016). Workplace learning is clearly hugely important to the information profession, not just because librarians act as teachers of others, but also because they are learners themselves. In order to teach others you need to be a lifelong learner, and for those working in the library sector continuing professional development has never been more important than it is now, with the rapid pace of change, driven largely by technology. A one-year Master's in librarianship or information studies really is only the foundation to becoming an information professional. Remember, many professionals (lawyers, doctors, nurses) study their craft for more than three years. Much of what librarians learn is 'on the job' and the changing pace of technology makes workplace learning vital. I've found the notion of communities of practice hugely helpful in understanding how librarians develop their own skills and knowledge and share what they think with colleagues and those in other institutions. Librarians are networked learners and in many ways a role model for other professionals and the notion of a community of practice is an important theme in workplace learning in this book.

As I said at the start, I was delighted to be asked to write this Foreword. This is a challenging book to read, but the selection of the chapters and the different voices that we hear make it a *compelling* read. We need to be constantly challenged to develop a deeper understanding of Information Literacy in all its guises and we need a critical and theoretical underpinning to our work as librarians and information professionals. In this book we have something to enlighten and challenge us, to reinforce what we already know, and tell us something new. The contributors include some writers who are shining lights in the Information Literacy field, such as Christine S. Bruce, Annemaree Lloyd, Bonnie Cheuk, Andrew Whitworth and Stéphane Goldstein. Each chapter offers us something new and valuable, but it is the sum of its parts that is the strength of this book and what make it such a rare treat. I hope you will read it and be enlightened, enthused and inspired.

Information Literacy really does have the power to transform people's lives and we see this particularly clearly in the workplace. The skills people develop at work impact on the success of the organizations that they work for, and on the economy and society more broadly. However, behaviours and knowledge can also be carried forward into daily lives, to enrich them, and as UNESCO says, enable them to fulfil both their personal and professional goals. There are new perspectives in this book but it is not before time that Information Literacy is recognized as something that transcends the education sector and has the power to underpin success in people's working and daily lives.

Jane Secker
London School of Economics and
Chair, CILIP Information Library Group

CHAPTER 1

Information Literacy and the workplace: new concepts, new perspectives?

Marc Forster

Introduction

As the focus of interest in Information Literacy (IL) continues to spread out from the university into the wider world, including the world of work, can we be confident that existing assumptions, definitions and methods of development continue to be relevant and appropriate? Both anecdotal and research evidence suggests not; that IL may not manifest as the same phenomenon in the workplace as it does in the academic environment. Young professionals, confronted by a way of dealing with information quite different to the academic, may be disorientated by the experience (Goldstein, 2014; Inskip, 2014; Williams, Cooper and Wavell, 2014; Osborn, 2011) and find themselves having to think about their relations to information in new ways: in terms of meaning, value, and purpose.

How is IL to be reconceptualized for the workplace? How should its parameters be redrawn so that librarians, academics, organizations and businesses can better understand workplace professionals and the students studying for those professions, and so effectively support them in efficient and creative engagement with the contemporary information landscape? How can IL be developed in a way that is meaningful and appropriate for them? Perhaps the question is one of evidence as much as conception. How can professions, many of which are especially focused on, and dependent on, information (Evetts, 2006) be supported in their information use if there is a lack of evidence as to how and why they use that information? Do we know in what ways information experiences in the workplace are significant to professionals themselves, their employers and educators and society at large? Indeed, what is the 'workplace' in an increasingly virtual information world?

Information Literacy's role and value in professional and workplace performance has been the subject of a number of recent research studies in the UK, Australia, Hong Kong and the USA. These studies have led to the development of new perspectives on workplace IL, including as a facilitator of effective and empowering inter-professional and professional–client relationships; as a component of the structure and dynamic of a 'learning' workplace, where decision making is therefore effective and creative; and as an ethical safeguard in the duty and responsibilities professionals have to clients, patients and employers to be fully informed when making vital decisions. This book includes discussions of key findings from these studies; new theories on how IL functions and manifests itself; and new methods for developing IL in professional groups, and fostering information-literate workplaces. All of this should be of value to library and information professionals as they attempt to survey the wide and complex workplace information horizon.

One of this book's principal aims, addressed in several chapters, is to help librarians, academics and information science students grasp the importance of understanding how IL is *experienced* by those professions they support and facilitate. The answer to the question of how IL is experienced addresses the knowledge 'gap' described above: how can library professionals know how, when and why information is used in the workplace? Such knowledge, potentially acquirable through appropriate research, shows how librarians can more profoundly engage with workplace professionals and their needs and ambitions. Using research evidence they can more precisely focus their information resource provision, potentially achieving both a superior service and a more cost-efficient one. There is also the possibility of more effective programmes of IL education, tailored as they could be to the information culture of the organization and the actual range and focus of the information experiences of workers. The continuing call for Evidence-based Practice in the library and information professions finds an echo here.

The contributors to this book have a particular interest in reaching the wider world of professional workers and their employers and educators. Helping members of these constituencies grasp the nature and value of IL as a key workplace attribute is vital for effective professional practice. In a world in which information is the very lifeblood of business and the professions, the quality of performance is dependent on the ability to use that information efficiently, effectively and creatively. Information illiteracy is potentially disastrous both for the individual professional and the employer. Hopefully the book will help promote awareness of IL's role in competence and Evidence-based Practice, self-development, teamworking and in achieving that ethical obligation to do the very best for patient or client – thus encouraging educators to integrate IL education into their courses, and showing them (and eventually their students) in what way it promotes effective workplace practice.

This introduction gives a brief overview of some key issues, problems and ideas discussed in each chapter. There is a wide range of perspectives, both international and UK-based, from the contributors, often with an extensive history of thinking and writing about Information Literacy; research methodology, research findings and organizational and individual perspectives are all discussed and put into context. As a result, styles of writing vary, but we have at all times tried to avoid too great a level of abstraction, though in some contexts abstraction is necessary (and hopefully illuminating!).

The workplace experience

Chapter 2 looks at ways in which librarians, academics and researchers have sought to understand the role of IL in the workplace and elsewhere. Behavioural and constructivist approaches have found favour over the years, and still have a useful role to play in thinking about the workplace. But *how, why and in what contexts* are the mental processes and actions that inform and constitute purposeful, effective and creative use of information put into practice in the workplace? How is IL actually experienced in the world of work? By looking at how IL is actually experienced in varying ways within differing work roles and contexts, librarians and other researchers are able to uncover, in a particularly detailed way, how it develops a professional's knowledge: the knowledge they need to perform such roles.

But how does one investigate IL experience? The chapter describes how interviews are conducted in such a way that experiences can be articulated clearly and accurately. Data analysis methods are described which produce a detailed picture of the whys and hows of IL experience, and the different roles and activities that are the contexts in which information is sought and knowledge developed.

Some researchers have come to the conclusion that IL experience always varies depending on context, and is always focused on developing the knowledge needed in that particular context. In the workplace, this implies IL allows a health, legal or business professional to work from an adequate basis of contextual, focused and purposeful knowledge so that the patient, client or customer has a good chance of receiving a fully competent and effective service. The information-literate professional life is, as Christine S. Bruce and colleagues have described, one of 'Informed Learning' (Bruce and Hughes, 2010).

Several chapters in this book are based to a greater or lesser extent on this 'relational' way of approaching IL; one that recognizes that it is experienced in different ways, depending on the differing contexts of workplace activity and the varying roles of the professional worker.

Information Literacy and the personal dimension

Chapter 3 uses the relational approach and information-knowledge-learning paradigm to look at IL as a 'personal' attribute. Information Literacy allows each individual to enrich the personal dimension of their work life. Through building relationships, through achieving and extending personal horizons, IL acts as a tool, and dimension, of the personality.

Information Literacy allows an employee to build on training and education to reach levels of higher competence and a wider information horizon. IL in the workplace also has a prominent *inter*-personal dimension. It allows the individual, operating in different roles, at different levels of complexity of experience, to contribute to a team or wider organization's knowledge aims and needs, or to work with clients or patients in a mutually beneficial exchange of information. The latter often involves the empowering of patients or clients or their families through relationships which involve sharing the information that can potentially inform key decisions about treatment, care or financial decision making. This use of information sharing as a conduit of intimacy and trust encourages patients or clients to release those intimate personal details that in turn can facilitate greater sensitivity in service or care.

The information-literate workplace

Information Literacy is a personal attribute, but can also be said to be an attribute of the workplace itself if its procedures and team structures facilitate the efficient and effective use of information sources in the creation of useable, contextual knowledge. In Chapter 4, Professors Mary M. Somerville and Christine S. Bruce give a vivid example of an application of the relational approach and information-knowledge-learning paradigm in the contemporary workplace. They illustrate how a workplace can be transformed for the better by using IL to inform its structures and relationships: an approach which has been given the name 'Informed Systems'. This approach aims to develop ways to facilitate continuous communication, decision making, action taking, and interactive evaluation processes through 'Informed Learning' experiences which catalyse and sustain relationships within the workplace that facilitate continuous inquiry and improvement. Through collaborative design, co-workers manage the flow of information to enable the organization to develop the knowledge it needs to flourish amidst dynamically changing circumstances. The leadership role is to foster purposeful inquiry relationships; such relationships create local information experiences that have the potential to transform the organization as a whole. Informed Systems advance collaborative evidence-based decision making: a key feature which will come to the fore frequently within the chapter. When framed as information-literate exchanges within a workplace, these experiences can, and do, transform processes for intuiting, interpreting, integrating, and institutionalizing knowledge. Leaders and managers will find particular value in this chapter about workplace revitalization.

The research and development that formed the framework for Informed Systems occurred in North American academic libraries, but the principles of collaborative and systemic IL derived from it are transferable to other contemporary workplace settings. It is clear from this initiative that it is possible for organizations to use information to take responsibility for creating their futures. The chapter offers readers an example of those processes which can lead us to understand how IL informs structures, processes and practices within a workplace.

In Chapter 5, Dr Elham Sayyad Abdi looks at that dimension of professional activity that transcends the workplace, through engagement with internet-wide communities of professional communication and practice. In professions in which such activity is an essential component, IL can be experienced through a range of contexts, which include workplace and professional community – its 'virtual' component. The chapter reviews the role of Virtuality in workplace IL experience. It considers how Virtuality enables IL to be experienced in a multidimensional and professionally enhanced way, perhaps suggesting a new theoretical construct for IL in the modern professions.

In Chapter 6 Stéphane Goldstein and Dr Andrew Whitworth ask the questions: How is IL valued in the workplace? What are the concrete benefits enterprises derive from recruiting, retaining and developing individuals who are information-literate? What returns on investment might be achieved in areas like providing information skills training to employees, developing new information-handling procedures, or even reconfiguring an office and going 'paperless'? What does the IL of employees, at all levels, add to the performance of enterprises? The chapter draws on the details of a funded project that sought to identify how IL contributes to a range of indicators of value for enterprises in the commercial, public and not-for-profit sectors, including organizational improvement, productivity, accountability and flexible or agile working. These indicators are mapped against five broad areas where enterprises make investments that relate to the use and handling of information and data. The chapter describes how the resulting correlation provides an analytical framework – which the project expressed through a practical tool – that enables enterprises to recognize how IL contributes to their corporate health.

In Chapter 10 (see also below, page 8), Dr Bonnie Cheuk describes how IL is intrinsic to workplace culture even if this is not recognized. She asks: if IL is important in the digital world, why don't we see the phrase appearing in job descriptions, or listed as an essential skill similar to communication skills, time management or project management? Dr Cheuk posits that IL is of value to any information-driven company and can often be found there. However, it is hidden within the contexts of business functionality; it is so embedded in the business activities that one cannot talk about it separately. Dr Cheuk suggests that IL models borrowed from the academic context are unlikely to meet the changing definition of information and the dynamic information needs of knowledge workers in different business contexts. A refined definition of IL in the workplace is put forward.

Best practice and Information Literacy's ethical role

Chapter 7 turns its attention to how Information Literacy contributes to professional norms of competence, effectiveness and fulfilment of the ethical necessity to achieve the best possible level of practice. To be an effective lawyer, doctor, nurse or social worker, or to work in the financial sector, is to deal each day with information. One must know when research evidence or other relevant legal, business, personal or other information is required, how to find it, how to critique it and how to integrate it into one's knowledge base. To fail to do so may result in defective practice. It follows that in some contexts to be information-illiterate qualifies as unethical practice, as failure to develop those competencies which allow one to operate from a complete knowledge base could have devastating consequences for clients or employers. In fact there seems to be an ethical requirement to go beyond mere competence in order to achieve the best outcome possible for the patient or client. IL appears from several research studies to have a role in the philosophical underpinning and practical processes of 'Evidence-based Practice', a form of best practice which explicitly focuses on the value of information in the form of complete, appropriate and contextualized research evidence. To be information-literate allows professionals to be aware of and able to locate, correctly interpret and apply research in a full and complete manner, in a way that promises to achieve the best outcome for their patient or client. 'Evidence' might be in the form of primary sources, such as papers discussing individual research studies or local data and personal client information, or secondary sources, such as professional guidelines and systematic reviews of research.

This is an uncommon way of looking at IL, but one vital to the understanding of its role in professional practice. It implies, amongst other things, that the acquisition of IL competencies has an ethical necessity. Does IL education emphasize this? The literature suggests not. Could it, however, be the means of driving forward IL education in the professions?

The development and promotion of Information Literacy

What of the educational, developmental perspective? Is IL valued in the workplace to the extent that its development is valued? How might librarians and others develop in professionals, and students studying for the professions, the information skills required in professional life?

In Chapter 8, Professor Annemaree Lloyd, a recognized international authority in IL and the workplace, provides an overall context and background to many of the issues around IL education and development. She discusses how the intensification of work and creation of new ways of working can present librarians with challenges. How can librarians develop IL education that provides the necessary 'scaffolding' for students' transitions into professional or vocational practice? Librarians must recast their teaching practices to accommodate characteristics of and developments in the nature of work. With this in mind, Professor Lloyd uses evidence from practice-based research to construct a conceptualization of workplace IL instruction.

In Chapter 9 Dr Stephen Roberts describes ways in which that scaffolding might be supported from an academic perspective. The chapter is an exploration of how higher orders of information professional competence can be introduced into programmes of higher education teaching and learning, with a view to deeper and wider dissemination across other professions and domains within the workplace, and their embedding within organizational learning and personal development.

The term 'information professional' (IP) has become an umbrella expression to denote the recognized educational and occupational focus for the qualified librarian, information manager, information services provider and knowledge manager and for those who work in the fields of documentation, records and archives. It has become a term that reflects the rise of an information-intensive society and the knowledge economy based not just on ICT and digital platforms but on wider social, behavioural and organizational changes with which these are linked. With a professional group so defined there is, due to its educational focus, an aspiration to engender a wider dispersion of higher order professional competences in information and knowledge work within other professionals in the workplace environment. Librarians, engaging with the contemporary information environment, can attempt to grasp the opportunity to propagate such roles and capacities more widely across other occupations and social groups in the workplace.

Dr Roberts revisits an initiative undertaken during the development of an MSc in Corporate Communication at the University of West London. An opportunity was identified in this business-focused and information- and communication-rich discipline for information professional academics to make an innovative contribution. A module was developed – 'Presenting Information Intelligence and Knowledge' (PIIK) – to provide a focus for introducing an information professional contribution to curriculum development and learning (Roberts, 2002; 2004). The module may suggest a model for developing information professional competences in disciplinary domains in a way which will facilitate the development of IL in the professions that seek their education in the university environment.

In Chapter 10, with a complementary perspective, Dr Bonnie Cheuk explores that wide range of workers who, although not necessarily described as such, are 'information and knowledge workers'. They deal with and disseminate information and knowledge, in different roles, functions and levels, under different operating models and company culture. She asks if and when IL adds value to a business, and if it does, how can information professionals play a business-driven, strategic yet pragmatic role to enhance those information and knowledge workers' IL capabilities. Despite the lack of acknowledgement and understanding of IL in the work world (see Chapter 6), many different roles within the workplace turn out to be information- and knowledge-focused. Information professionals can be more broadly defined as key employees of whatever label who have to consciously consider how best to help the company leverage information and/or create information systems, services and marketplaces to create value for employers, clients or business stakeholders. A practical case study is put forward to illustrate how a global company might successfully roll out an IL programme disguised as a 'change management' programme within a broader culture-change initiative.

There have been several attempts in recent years to put forward an evidence-based, 'relational' form of IL education, made possible through the use of research techniques that provide descriptions of the *range* of IL experiences within a particular group or profession. This has been given additional development through the 'Experience Framework' described in Chapter 11, formulated from a more detailed analysis of the range of contexts and levels of complexity of experience of IL in a relevant group or profession. Groupings of aspects of that experience are used to formulate highly practice-focused and detailed scenario-based educational interventions through the application of Variation Theory, an education theory developed from previous research. Such evidence-based methods have the highest probability of developing IL in the workplace, and also of reinforcing its perceived relevance for professionals and their employers, based as they are on actual workplace experiences.

One of the recurrent problems in IL education is how 'progress' can be assessed and monitored meaningfully. Are the skills or knowledge domains that are usually assessed the key ones? Also discussed in Chapter 11 is a new experience-focused means of monitoring the growth of IL that has been developed in the context of the research described above. The method is especially useful in the wide-ranging and complex information world of the workplace.

The workplace is a context in which approaches to IL beyond the well established academic or library-focused ones are needed. Although research into IL experience in the workplace still has a long way to go, it has already yielded much of value. We hope that you find the new and developing approaches, initiatives and ideas discussed in the following chapters thought-provoking and seminal.

CHAPTER 2

How is Information Literacy experienced in the workplace?

Marc Forster

This chapter will discuss:

- how researchers have sought to understand Information Literacy (IL), including how it is 'experienced' in the real world.
- how IL can be understood as something experienced in a range of contexts meaningful to the individual and relevant to her/his contributive engagement with the workplace.
- how IL experience can be investigated to show the kinds of purposeful knowledge development activities that it facilitates and that are key to the functioning workplace.

Introduction

According to the information theoretician Luciano Floridi, knowledge is information which is both significant and true in its meaning (Floridi, 2010); a sufficiency of which, when brought into relationship with existing knowledge (learning), leads to increased understanding and more effective decision making (Megill, 2012; Hoyt, Bailey and Yoshihashi, 2012). Information Literacy operates at the information–knowledge crux: seeking, sorting, evaluating information; managing and presenting true information within new structures and relationships of knowledge. It is experienced by someone who can 'synthesis[e] . . .. information and data to create new knowledge' (SCONUL, 2011, 11) and so promote learning.

The findings derived from a study of the experience of IL in the nursing profession (Forster 2015a) appeared to show that IL is always an experience of the development of the knowledge, and hence the knowledge-based decision-making abilities, that nurses need in the specific contexts of their practice. The findings from this study, together with an analysis of the findings of several previous studies in IL experience (e.g. Boon, Johnston and Webber, 2007; Diehm and Lupton, 2012; Williams, 2007; Lloyd, 2006; Lupton, 2008; Limberg, 1999; Yates, Partridge and Bruce, 2009), as well as consideration of recent work by Bruce and various colleagues (Bruce and Hughes, 2010; Bruce, Hughes and Somerville, 2012), suggested that this may be true of IL experience in general. IL experience always appears to involve the development of knowledge that is meaningful in specific contexts. In the workplace, IL experiences generate the knowledge that contributes to a greater understanding, and to the successful undertaking, of designated roles and tasks (Forster, 2015a). Such experiences include an awareness of the information required in each workplace context, and the varying sources, processes and 'co-participatory practices' (Lloyd, 2010) needed to develop knowledge as the context varies. This implies a key role for IL in the facilitation of health, legal, business or other professional engagement in those knowledge development and learning processes which allow practitioners to achieve competence and effective practice. The potential practical value of this understanding and approach to IL will be discussed in various contexts within this book.

The nursing study will be used for example purposes throughout several chapters of this book. Its methodological structure (as we will see) allowed a wide range of conclusions about such experiences to be drawn which could be reasonably applied to the workplace generally, especially where professionals worked in teams, had clients or patients, and had an obligation to those clients or patients to work from the highest possible level of knowledge and informed practice. Where appropriate, other studies will be referred to; however, studies of professional IL experiences of sufficient detail remain small in number.

This chapter will begin by briefly looking at some of the ways IL has been studied and understood and their value in the workplace context. The nature and significance of IL experience, and how such experience might be investigated in a workplace, is then discussed.

Ways of thinking about Information Literacy

There have been several ways of thinking about and investigating information Literacy since the introduction of the concept in 1974. Early approaches understood it as a complex of skills and knowledge by means of which one finds and uses information effectively. Others took a more subjective view, focusing on 'competence' within contexts of information use (Snavely and Cooper, 1997) and regarding IL as a personal attribute. A later approach embraced the idea of IL as something experienced in the real world – in technical terms, a 'phenomenon'. This latter approach allows us to draw a picture of what IL is 'for' and how and why it functions as part of day-to-day work life. Specifically it shows us what kinds of knowledge a worker needs, and how information is used to develop it.

Do such approaches dictate how we see the value, significance and pervasiveness of IL in the modern work environment? It is certainly true that researchers, librarians, managers/entrepreneurs and professionals can be affected by how they conceptualize, investigate and value it. The value of investigating IL 'experience' is that such an approach is more likely to give us the 'reality' of IL experience that can be so useful to librarians and employers.

Skills and knowledge in the workplace

From the earliest days of its conceptualization, IL has been seen in its 'simplest' form as a range of uncontextualized abilities in the form of *skills* in the use of information search tools, and application of *knowledge* needed to use these tools effectively and make sense of the information found (Doyle, 1992). In the workplace this may mean skilful use of company websites or other electronic databases or resources designed for particular professions, such as Lexis/Nexis for lawyers or Business Source Premier. Students training for the professions are usually taught how to use these tools and how to interpret what they find; and employers may expect, if not all their employees, at least those in key positions with an instructional or information dissemination role, to be proficient. In this model of IL, information searches can be planned and executed, and information of value can be retrieved, critiqued and 'applied', by following standard processes and applying abstract knowledge, in any given context; the fundamental experience being the same in each case. To what end and in what context the information is sought and applied is irrelevant.

However, one may ask: are purpose and context significant in the proper understanding of IL in the workplace? In order to understand and develop IL do we need to know more of its contextual purpose, functionality and value? Perhaps such knowledge might allow us to show relevant stakeholders the value of its development?

Knowing how to use information in context

Some approaches to IL are 'constructivist'. That is, IL is a personal attribute (SCONUL, 2011), the ability to apply skills and knowledge to solve a problem in the real world (Kuhlthau, 1988; 2004). Knowing how to search databases and critique findings is not enough; the information-literate person must be able to exhibit an ability to reflect and so adapt information practices. One must know what information is required under which circumstances to solve which specific knowledge-deficit 'problems'. Considering the value that is therefore placed on knowing how skills and knowledge are applied in practice, it is not surprising that this should be an approach valued in workplace IL analysis and research. Scenario-based IL education for health and social care workers is based on an understanding that information is used in context and for particular purposes. Those numerous purposes, derived from the multifaceted nature of the workplace environment, determine how, when and why information is required and used. Therefore to be effective in the workplace requires training in the relationship between information and its contexts of use, including what information is used *for*.

It is understood from this perspective that necessary skills and knowledge might change significantly between contexts and purposes and in themselves have no absolute value as markers of IL. However, several questions remain: 'what is the actual nature of each context in terms of IL experience?'; 'how does IL actually exhibit in each context?'; and 'does each context always elicit the same IL experiences?' amongst others.

Information Literacy from an organizational perspective

Although Information Literacy definition and research is often focused on the individual, and this is relevant to workplaces in which individuals operate in professional and other responsible roles, much interest in IL in the workplace is focused on the 'information-literate organization'. How do organizations expect their employees to use and share information, and to what ends? How do individuals share information within teams and how do organizations co-ordinate information flow from various internal and external sources? In fact, how do organizations develop a general knowledge base? Lloyd (2010) and others insist that workplace IL is strongly team-focused, with 'individual' information use less common. Some of the chapters in this book will take such perspectives, either entirely or in part, and from a constructivist or relational/experiential perspective. Each of these perspectives can, and have, been employed to informative effect.

In an organizational context, interest lies in how the organization deals with information in order to perform necessary activities, and how IL in individuals and team structures contributes to this. However, the details of 'knowledge management', the process of finding and effectively using organizational knowledge, are outside the scope of this book.

Real-world experiences

Some researchers were unsatisfied with what they were able to discover about IL and how it operated in the real world, including that of the workplace.

How were the processes and actions that constituted information skills and knowledge actually experienced? Where and when did the information-literate person engage with information and why? Hjørland's approach to information-seeking behaviour (Hjørland, 2000) suggested that IL could be seen as a sequence of processes and behaviours experienced in, and given meaning by, the 'information world' in which the individual operates. IL was something experienced in different ways and contexts meaningful to the individual and relevant to their significant engagement with their world.

Meaningful and relevant in what way? Research (Forster, 2015a) suggested meaningful and relevant to the individual's attempt to function effectively in the activities and roles that made up that engagement; roles that, in many contexts but especially that of the workplace, implied the need for information that could be turned into knowledge. In simple terms, IL was a tool for contextual learning; for 'making sense' (Cheuk and Dervin, 2011) to practical effect.

Using terms commonly employed in information science, we can develop this further and attempt a definition of the experience of IL in the workplace:

> Information Literacy in the workplace is learning, experienced as task-focused information need and its fulfilment through effective information engagement as knowledge development, ontologically grounded in a discourse community and its domain.

Information science literature often refers to a profession as a *discourse community*: a group with a common purpose and a commonly understood means of communication (Swales, 1990) all of which takes place within, and by means of, its information world or 'domain'. A 'domain' is 'the set of information systems, resources, services and processes associated with a group of users with common concerns' (Bawden and Robinson, 2012, 93). Information need, search, critique and application are given context and relationship, performed as they are under impulses derived from a discourse community (such as a particular profession) whose knowledge structures are to be acquired, interpreted, developed and employed. An individual's IL experience in the workplace is grounded in the interlinked workplace and professional communities and their information domains, experience that varies by an individual's role, purpose and, of course, pre-existing knowledge and understanding. Lloyd (2010) has used the expression 'Information Literacy landscape' to describe the unity of the discourse community and domain.

Investigating Information Literacy experience in the workplace
A methodology for investigating Information Literacy experience
Finding the meanings and contexts of IL experiences of a profession or other

work-based group promises valuable information on how they might be supported by librarians in terms of information resources provision and IL education. If we know how and why, in what context, information is used, we can understand what information resources must be made available by a library and information service, and the information activities that need to be understood, taught and facilitated.

So how might IL experience be investigated? Researchers have made use of a qualitative methodology, phenomenography, for this purpose. The term phenomenography is defined by its founder as:

> The empirical study of the limited number of qualitatively different ways in which various phenomena in, and aspects of, the world around us are experienced.
>
> Marton, 1994, 4424

Researchers interview participants using lightly structured interview protocols, encouraging them to expand on their experiences of using information and focusing on those which they themselves regard as significant (making sure not to impose the interviewer's ideas of what is significant). Rather than asking participants to give their definition of Information Literacy, they are asked to describe when they sought and applied information effectively to increase purposeful knowledge in their day-to-day lives. Hence 'data' is rich in the experiences of the concept of IL, even for those participants unfamiliar with it.

Analysis of the interview transcripts eventually yields descriptions of the archetypal ways in which the group experience IL, which are believed to reflect that of the original population as a whole. These 'Categories of Description', when taken together, give the overall picture of the ways in which the original population (such as a profession) experience IL. Each category does not represent a subgroup; any individual could experience being information-literate in any of the ways described, depending on the context and purpose of information need.

This kind of research has provided some useful information about how groups experience things: for example, that the range and variation in how something is experienced within a group or population is limited and not, as might be imagined, infinite; that the variations can be described in a simple descriptive way; and that the variations can be linked in an informative way, often as a hierarchy of complexity of experience.

In some studies, such as the type described in detail below, the archetypal experiences described by Categories of Description are in a form which points to the nature of the knowledge that experiencing IL generates. It is this insight into what a group learns through IL, and in what contexts, that has the potential to allow IL education to be focused more effectively, and so in due course develop more effective professional and workplace information use. Chapter 11 gives an example of how this might be done.

Christine S. Bruce (Bruce, 1997) was the first to use phenomenography to investigate IL. From her research into Australian academics, she derived seven Categories of Description describing the ways in which they experience being information-literate. The relational model of Information Literacy developed from this study emphasizes that the information user's experience of being information-literate is subjective but contextualized. Each individual can potentially experience IL in any of the ways described by the categories, exchanging one way for another as their perspective, and their information behaviour, changes; although not all information users are necessarily capable of the more complex experiences.

This 'relational' approach to IL has begun to find mainstream recognition. From ACRL's (American College and Research Libraries) recent re-assessment of their definition of Information Literacy:

> ACRL's previous definition of information literacy describes it as a set of skills or competencies that are uniform among all learners . . . Other conceptions growing out of the research of Bruce, Lupton, Lloyd, and Limburg [sic] identify the limitations of this skill- and- individual-attribute-based conception . . . [and] emphasize [instead] the highly relational, context-specific nature of information literacy.
> ACRL, 2014, 4

Bruce's work has proven to be seminal. Since 1997 other studies have investigated the experience of IL in specific groups and contexts. Some of these studies have gone on to draw further conclusions about IL, including conclusions significant to the work environment. These include the idea that IL is, at its centre, the key to knowledge development and so to learning. 'Information literacy is about effective engagement with information, when learning in different contexts' (Bruce and Hughes, 2010, A2).

Conducting an investigation into Information Literacy experience

Data collection

As mentioned above, data collection is conducted through semi-structured interviews with

> the researcher clearly setting the interview topic through the use of a number of set questions, but then making substantial use of follow-up questions to further investigate interviewees' responses
> Åkerlind, Bowden and Green, 2005, 80

in order to encourage the participant to freely describe their experiences of IL in a manner which reveals the range of meanings it has for them in their 'world', while avoiding imposing the researcher's assumptions, either conscious or unconscious.

It is essential that interview questions are as open-ended as possible (Marton, 1988) to allow the participant to be free to express in full what IL means to them: what information is used for and what knowledge is needed in their day-to-day work lives. The interview should also be flexible in terms of direction and question order for the same purpose. There should not be too many questions with too many details of the questions developed in advance. Questions should follow and be in the context of what the participant is saying and is currently describing. The interviewer must develop follow-up questions which respond to the participant's own handling of the questions and corresponding exposition of those experiences.

It is important for the validity of the research that interviewees are allowed to describe experiences freely, without guidance or suggestion.

Data analysis

The interviews are recorded and an accurate transcript of each is produced.

The data analysis method has several stages (Åkerlind, 2005). The process begins with careful analysis of the transcripts to identify examples, and develop descriptions, of experiences of using information that are common to at least some of the participants.

After development of these descriptions there is a process of *categorization*: both 'vertically', bringing together experiences of varying complexity under several 'themes' that describe the different ways how and why information is sought and used by the group, and 'horizontally', bringing together experiences (from all themes) describing the same level of complexity. As we'll see below, this latter 'horizontal' process allows us to make general descriptions (Categories of Description) of the roles in the workplace that 'fit' each particular complexity level of information activity: for example, the role that employs a range of simple day-to-day activities in which basic immediate knowledge is required, and at the other extreme the more senior roles that employ deep and wide-ranging experiences in which knowledge is developed to allow strategic thinking to take place.

These initial descriptions of experience, and the structures developed from them, are the 'outcome' or 'results' of the research study, providing a detailed and valuable description of the how, when and why the group uses information.

The data analysis process in detail

Sorting and analysing the transcripts

1 **The process begins** with an initial engagement with the transcripts of the interviews. This is a process which develops increasing levels of familiarity to the point where the researcher can begin identifying, within and across the transcripts, describable information experiences: descriptions of how or why information was used in the workplace. Each transcript is read through three times; on the third reading notes are made, describing and summarizing these impressions.

2 **The next stage** involves grouping transcripts together after re-reading both the transcripts and the notes several times. What are the main themes? How and why (in a general way at this stage) is information understood, sought and used, and how can these experiences be described? 'How' might be: *searching professional databases*; 'Why' might be: *facilitating relationships; attempting to achieve competent working practice; contributing to a team*. A transcript might appear in several groups if several of these themes are prominent.

3 **The next stage** involves rearranging the groups after further readings, and focusing on the 'why' and 'how' more closely, at a finer level of detail, in order to develop 'Dimensions of Variation of Awareness'. These are simple statements which describe experience of IL, the seeking, critiquing and using of information, for a *particular* purpose in work life; a more focused 'why' or 'how'. These are the building blocks from which we can construct descriptions of how our group of information users experience IL as a profession.

Developing the building blocks

1 **The process of developing Dimensions of Variation** begins with the identification and underlining of statements which seem to describe or suggest IL experience which focuses on a specific 'why' or 'how' of the kind described above. These are labelled by means of brief words or phrases describing the experience's context, e.g. 'finding information for client families' or 'contributing to the multidisciplinary team' or 'searching for clinical guidelines'.

2 **The next stage** is to seek links in meaning and significance to *other* apparently related statements elsewhere in the transcript. This is a more complex process than simply looking for similarities of phrasing; it involves seeking expressions which might suggest a further development, modification or focusing of the original description is necessary. If such expressions are found, the original descriptive identifier is modified accordingly.

3   **This process continues across the other transcripts from the same group**. If the experience is traced in other transcripts then the process of modification of the expression is continued. The expression continues to be modified until it satisfactorily expresses the experience of the wider group (or at least some of it).

How does this work in practice? Here are two examples (Forster, 2015a):

Example 1: How the dimension of variation *Information Literacy experienced in developing an evidence-based ward culture* was formulated

This evolved, to begin with, from descriptions of experiences involving the location and application of research evidence which were underlined and compared. These were found to often be contextualized in the transcripts by a sense of professionalism and conviction. Elsewhere, both within the same transcript and in others, this was further developed by some participants in discussions of the need for the wider adoption of such attitudes within the profession; of how their information activities encouraged colleagues to use research evidence and think in an evidence-based way; and how they themselves have through their information activities contributed to Evidence-based Practice's entrenchment within their team and ward.

Example 2: How the dimension of variation *Achieving optimum and so ethically defensible care* was formulated

Initial statements describing searching for, and applying research evidence in both primary and secondary form, occurred in contexts in which it was made clear by participants that Evidence-based Practice was an attempt to achieve the best possible care. This was frequently contextualized in discussions of responsibilities to patients and the nature of those responsibilities. These discussions often referred to the negative consequences of failure to be information-literate in this way; consequences which could be harmful for patients and therefore gave an ethical colouring to IL.

This 'iterative' process is key to validity (Åkerlind, Bowden and Green, 2005).

Developing structures from the building blocks
Themes of Expanding Awareness

The themes or general 'why's and 'how's of IL experience can be understood as 'parts' of the overall experience, the sum total of which (there can be anywhere from three to eight of them) describes IL experience as a whole. Themes of the 'why' type within workplace IL experience might include: organizational or personal decision making, collaborative design, Evidence-based Practice, disciplinary research, professional and private problem solving (Bruce, 2008; 2012).

The technical term used is 'theme of expanding awareness': a name which highlights the other dimension within IL experience: higher or lower levels of complexity. Complexity of experience reflects 'awareness' of IL's potentialities, of what it is capable of; or what it needs to do. Experiences may be simple ones in which information is used in simple day-to-day tasks or more complex, in which information is used for activities, for instance, at a strategic level.

The themes are derived initially from the 'grouping of transcripts' stage of the sorting and analysing process, and are refined and finalized through the process of grouping the Dimensions of Variation under them. The process is completed when we can:

- arrange all of the dimensions under themes, and each theme gives a satisfactory general description of its group of dimensions
- arrange all of the dimensions within each theme in order of complexity, from least complex experience to most complex (the 'vertical' grouping mentioned at the beginning of this data analysis section).

These processes rely on objective judgement which requires correction or confirmation by others. This is important for the validity of the research outcome.

In our examples above, the Dimensions of Variation *Developing an evidence-based ward culture* and *Achieving optimum and so ethically defensible care* were both grouped under the theme 'Information Literacy experienced through its role in helping to achieve "best practice"'. The latter was judged to be a slightly more sophisticated experience than the former.

Categories of Description

The next structural formulations are the *Categories of Description*. These are developed from the grouping and summary description of the **Dimensions from all of the Themes**, hence from the whole breadth of IL experience, *at the same comparative level of sophistication of experience* (the 'horizontal' grouping).

This can best be understood clearly by means of the diagram in Figure 2.1 on the next page.

A range of Categories of Description which describe a 'way of experiencing Information Literacy' are produced in this way, with the level of complexity of experience varying from simple to very complex – in workplace terms, from simple day-to-day tasks to those at the strategic level. The number of themes and categories will vary between studied populations.

An example of a research study into Information Literacy experience

The nursing study, which made use of the methods described above, found

	Categories of description					
Themes	**A**	**B**	**C**	**D**	**E**	**F**
1	Dimensions of lowest complexity	Dimensions of greater complexity	Dimensions of greater complexity still	Dimensions	Dimensions	Dimensions of highest complexity
2	Dimensions of lowest complexity	Dimensions of greater complexity	Dimensions of greater complexity still	Dimensions	Dimensions	Dimensions of highest complexity
3	Dimensions of lowest complexity	Dimensions of greater complexity	Dimensions of greater complexity still	Dimensions	Dimensions	Dimensions of highest complexity
4	Dimensions of lowest complexity	Dimensions of greater complexity	Dimensions of greater complexity still	Dimensions	Dimensions	Dimensions of highest complexity
5	Dimensions of lowest complexity	Dimensions of greater complexity	Dimensions of greater complexity still	Dimensions	Dimensions	Dimensions of highest complexity
6	Dimensions of lowest complexity	Dimensions of greater complexity	Dimensions of greater complexity still	Dimensions	Dimensions	Dimensions of highest complexity
7	Dimensions of lowest complexity	Dimensions of greater complexity	Dimensions of greater complexity still	Dimensions	Dimensions	Dimensions of highest complexity

Expanding 'awareness' of complexity of potential experience →

Figure 2.1 *Relationship between dimensions, themes and Categories of Description*

that IL was experienced under seven themes. That is, there are seven general 'why's and 'how's describing IL experience in nursing practice, under which 70 Dimensions of Variation, the more specific and focused 'why's and 'how's, could be grouped in order of complexity:

1 Information Literacy experienced in processes of professional self-development
2 Information Literacy experienced in development and maintenance of relationships (with patients, patients' families, colleagues and other professionals)
3 Information Literacy experienced through its role in helping to achieve best practice
4 Information Literacy experienced within understandings and experiences of Evidence-based Practice
5 Information Literacy experienced within application of skills and processes of evidence and other information gathering
6 Information Literacy experienced in the context of an understanding and knowledge of the principles and concepts behind evidence and other information gathering
7 Information Literacy experienced through applicable conceptions of information.

The Dimensions of Variation under, for example, Theme 3 could be arranged in six groups, each of similar complexity, labelled A to F and given a summary description, 'A' gathering the least complex experiences and 'F' the most complex. This is a helpful process when there are as many dimensions as there are in this study; it both encourages close analysis by the researcher of the dimensions and makes the process of the creation of Categories of Description easier.

The dimensions themselves are bullet-pointed:

A Practising with sufficient background information to function:
  • obtaining sufficient background psycho-socio-cultural background knowledge on a patient
  • determining the most cost-effective/efficient treatment option.
B Helping the team practice efficiently:
  • contributing evidence and other information to the multidisciplinary team.
C Using information as a tool for 'improvement':
  • attempting to improve individual outcomes
  • attempting to 'improve my practice'
  • suggesting a change in practice.

D   Working towards an effective practice dynamic:
   • developing up-to-date practice
   • developing practice that is recognized as objectively proven/justifiable
   • developing rationales for change.
E   Developing a culture of efficiency and accountability:
   • developing a culture of change within the ward
   • developing a culture of accountability to patients
   • developing an evidence-based ward culture.
F   Exploring the compassionate and ethical foci of care:
   • exploring the parameters of compassionate care
   • focusing on the nature of patient safety
   • achieving optimum and so ethically defensible care.

Six Categories of Description were identified: Category A (the simplest experience) through to Category F (the most complex).

Category A was developed from the groups of dimensions under each theme that described the simplest experiences:

• from Theme 1: seeking out basic knowledge of clinical contexts and conditions
• from Theme 2: interacting passively with others – others as a source of information
• from Theme 3: practising with sufficient background information to function
• from Theme 4: obtaining instruction in seeking to understand the process of care
• from Theme 5: operating with limited negotiation of the technology
• from Theme 6: using background technical knowledge of information sources and types, needed to find and use evidence
• from Theme 7: working with the 'basic facts'.

Bringing these into a unity gives an overall picture of one way (in this case the simplest way) of experiencing IL as a nurse. We can describe this way of experiencing in the form of a role. How can we describe the role of a nurse who experiences IL in this least complex form? Category A: **the passive minimalist**. This nurse obtains 'the facts' to deal with the immediate and simple issue or context. Passive information absorption occurs as frequently as information gathering; the latter may frequently be of the 'scavenging' type.

The other categories were:

B   **the knowledgeable goal achiever** (creating knowledge for specific goals)

C **the focused, competent and evolving professional** (creating knowledge to develop professional competence – to function effectively in particular day-to-day roles)
D **the confident and trusted promoter of justifiable change** (creating knowledge that can be used as an agent of change through an understanding of situations and contexts)
E **the teacher and promoter of an evidence-based culture** (developing knowledge infrastructures which allow specific roles to be performed of the kind which must be based on a complete or almost complete understanding of a context or activity)
F **the leader, philosopher and strategist** (developing knowledge infrastructures which allow one to act as an established source or vector of 'wisdom' in various specific contexts).

The nurse can potentially move between the different ways of experiencing IL depending on the immediate context. She may be a *passive minimalist* in some contexts of her work and a *teacher and promoter of an evidence-based culture* in others.

Information Literacy as task-focused knowledge development

What about other studies of IL experience?

Earlier in the chapter we defined IL in the workplace in this way:

> Information Literacy in the workplace is learning, experienced as task-focused information need and its fulfilment through effective information engagement as knowledge development, ontologically grounded in a discourse community and its domain.

Though the Categories of Description in the nursing study all contained aspects of experience which were processes related to information gathering (the 'how's, from Themes 5, 6 and 7), the categories also incorporate aspects (the 'why's, from Themes 1–4) which focused the complete experience on, and in, the *development of knowledge required for particular clinical functions*; that is, the development of knowledge as needed to function in the workplace. This was something which seemed particularly significant.

That all of the 'complete' experiences of IL were focused on knowledge development might seem obvious. How else would IL express itself in the real world but in a successful attempt to develop one's subjective knowledge or the knowledge of a team through the effective acquisition and use of information? However, this idea of IL hasn't been a universally accepted one, especially by those who focus their understanding on behaviourist paradigms. What about the rest of the research literature into 'Information Literacy experience'? Do other research studies point to the same conclusion? Could the statement 'Information Literacy experiences are always focused on purposeful knowledge development' be supported by the findings of previous work?

Most other studies in IL experience (e.g. Boon, Johnston and Webber, 2007; Diehm and Lupton, 2012; Williams, 2007; Lloyd, 2006; Lupton, 2008; Limberg, 1999; Yates, Partridge and Bruce, 2009) can be summarized as producing Categories of Description of three types:

1 'Process' categories in which experience is focused on Information skills and competence. Categories entirely of the 'how' aspect of IL.
2 'Knowledge' categories, in which the experience is clearly marked as developing knowledge. Knowledge of something for a particular purpose.
3 Knowledge-based decision-making categories, in which knowledge is developed to enable effective decision making, teaching or similar knowledge-backed creative activities.

Categories of Description of types 2 and 3 clearly support the idea that IL is focused on the development of knowledge. Type 1 categories, apparently, contradict this. These 'process' categories don't seem to be focused in this way. They have a 'how' aspect but not a 'why'. However, such categories seem to be reinterpretable based on the findings of the nursing study.

As we have seen, the nursing study showed that complete experiences of IL as described by the Categories of Description consisted of all seven of its themes. Some of these themes, primarily numbers 5, 6 and 7, had functional or 'how' characteristics – that is, were focused on the information identification and gathering itself. However, these functional experiences of IL were always partial ones and always formed part of a complete experience focused on personal knowledge development, as defined and contextualized by the Categories of Description.

This view of Categories of Description as containing several aspects, including necessarily both functional and meaning-focused ones, 'how' and 'why', is supported by the philosopher Edmund Husserl's analysis of the essential nature of the experience of phenomena (Cerbone, 2006). Husserl described such experience as a composite of an awareness of process (or what he labelled 'noetic' themes, which describe the 'activity across time' component of the experience of a phenomenon) and an awareness of meaning ('noematic' themes). Experiences must have meaning as well as functionality – must have a 'why' aspect and a 'how' aspect. That meaning, in the experience of IL, is the knowledge developed for the purposes experienced in the context of that experience.

The unique detail of the nursing study's analysis methods, absent from previous studies, allows us to see that Type 1 categories aren't complete descriptions of IL at all.

Informed Learning

Information Literacy experience in the workplace is . . . creating knowledge to operate competently, to maintain relationships, to develop personally, to lead, to create . . . and to learn.

The idea that IL is key to knowledge development and learning is increasingly finding favour:

> Information literacy is . . . the use of information in **creating new knowledge** and participating ethically in communities of learning.
>
> ACRL, 2015, 3

If this is indeed the case, then IL can be seen as an aspect of the learning or sense making process. In the context of the workplace, it can be seen as the means through which employees develop both their own team's as well as their customers' or clients' knowledge in ways which help them contribute to the organization's aims.

An awareness of the nature and context of IL experiences is vital. Research which allows organizations, and the information professionals who work for them, to know and understand just how, why and in what contexts IL promotes knowledge development and learning in a workplace, team or profession and why, might improve workplace effectiveness and allow librarians to better focus their IL education and information resources provision.

Conclusion

Bruce and colleagues have developed from this understanding of IL as context focused knowledge development, the concept of 'Informed Learning' (Bruce and Hughes, 2010; Bruce, Hughes and Somerville, 2012), in which IL's role within learning is described and made explicit as:

> . . . using information to learn. It . . . is about being aware of the kinds of information we are using, how we are using information and how different forms of information come together to inform and transform our work.
>
> Bruce, Hughes and Somerville, 2012, 8–9

Informed Learning is based on the belief, derived from research into the experience of IL in varying environments (Bruce and Hughes, 2010), that IL is an engine which propels learning (individually and collectively), through awareness of the ways in which information can be used to build knowledge in the workplace, amongst other environments. IL is something experienced in, and transferable to, a range of contexts and purposes, and is fundamental to the learning process as a 'transformative' generator of knowledge (Bruce, Hughes and Somerville, 2012).

Importantly, workplace IL, when transformed into Informed Learning through knowledge of contextual experiences, is team-focused and inter-professional. It facilitates collaboration in which knowledge development is focused on the team's, and organization's, aims and priorities.

These ideas and approaches are helpful in the analysis of IL in the workplace. They highlight the contextuality of IL and therefore of the development of knowledge and learning (Bruce, Hughes and Somerville, 2012). They identify IL as the motor of learning and therefore central to effectiveness in those workplaces which feature professions in which information gathering and interpretation are fundamental (Evetts, 2006). They imply that IL allows a health, legal or business professional to work from an adequate basis of knowledge so that the patient, client or customer receives a fully competent and creative service.

The study of IL experience can shed light on the information-focused learning processes and contexts which occur in every workplace or professional collaboration involving individual, team and interactive information use. If those learning contexts are highlighted and learning processes are understood, then it becomes possible to assist the individual and team to greater awareness and understanding of the best ways to use information to learn in ways that contribute to the organization's goals. Librarians can be key to the learning process, not only within the education setting, but also within the work setting. They can do this not only as developers of information knowledge and skills, but through developing awareness of context, potential fields of information activity and how such skills might be contextually applied to professional and organizational effect, as well as which information resources are essential to professional activity. Research evidence is the key.

Information Literacy and the personal dimension: team players, empowered clients and career development

Marc Forster

This chapter will discuss:

- how Information Literacy (IL) helps each professional to develop and find scope for their personal capabilities, and facilitates the relationships which enable them to support and empower clients or patients and contribute in team and organizational contexts.
- how research can allow us to observe those experiential meanings and professional information horizons that illuminate IL at a personal level.

Introduction

Information Literacy can be seen as a personal attribute: one which, as a facilitator and enricher of the communicative faculty, can aid a professional to assist and empower patients or clients, and make a personal contribution to mutual endeavours within team and business or organization by supporting, leading or teaching colleagues.

It also facilitates the *development* of personal capabilities through its ability to facilitate learning (Bruce and Hughes, 2010), and therefore to engage in new and more sophisticated ways to make a contribution.

These perspectives on IL are essential to the understanding of its role and value in the workplace. That workplace is often a very complex social environment which is focused on the use of information for specific knowledge goals, often with and for the benefit of patients and clients, and often through teams and networks undertaking complex knowledge-generating tasks. The sections below are intended to help information professionals, library managers and academics responsible for education in the professions become more aware of some of the likely details of IL's personal and social complexities and value, in order to support professionals in training and in the workplace as they negotiate their information world; '*likely* details' because, though most professionals will share many of these experiences, further research into specific workplaces and professions is still required for absolute clarity.

What the research data can show

Knowledge of the breadth and depth of experience of IL can give valuable perspectives on how individuals, at different levels of responsibility, make their personal contribution to the development of knowledge needed by the team and organization, and the patients or clients they have responsibility for. How does IL allow them to make their own unique contribution in the workplace? In what way does it facilitate relationships with others? Does it inform leadership or form the basis for personal development? If so, how? The answers to these questions may be valuable to those who are responsible for IL education, and professional education in general.

As we saw in Chapter 2, research (Forster, 2015a) has shown that the experience of being information-literate in a particular profession or group can be resolved into 'themes' which together make up the whole breadth of its experience. The themes are a mixture of 'meaning' and 'process'; the former describing *why* information has meaning for the individual in this context (i.e. what is the knowledge required and why is it required?). Later sections will show that the range of 'personal' meanings, in areas such as personal development and relationship dynamics, available to members of a group or profession in their information world can be described.

Such studies also yield 'categories of description', representing and describing variations in the experience of IL across all themes. The several categories, whether using the method described in Chapter 2 or not (Bruce, 1997, Boon, Johnston and Webber, 2007; Andretta, 2010; Forster, 2015a), are often distinguished from each other by the progressively more complex ways in which information is applied and resultant knowledge used. The level of complexity of IL experience an individual requires, or is capable of, can determine and facilitate, amongst other things, the nature of relationships with clients, colleagues and the wider organization. Their 'information horizon' described by the categories might be limited to employing simple facts to fulfil basic tasks for a client or colleague, or involve a wider perspective in which complex analyses and detailed reports and research projects are used in leadership contexts and roles which require 'blue-sky thinking' and strategic abilities. All of these roles exist in the context of client/patient relationships and/or teams or wider organizations, or indeed are combinations of all.

Broader organizational contexts, such as those described by Cheuk in

Chapter 10 and Goldstein and Whitworth in Chapter 6, and studies which deal with personal experience, together suggest how future research into IL in the workplace may have two different directions and perspectives: the organizational ('information-literate organizations' which give the context for individual roles) and the 'personal' (individual IL experience which informs the dynamics of the 'information-literate team'). If both approaches were used, an 'Information Literacy audit' might be possible: a multi-perspective analysis of an organization's information-use dynamic.

The information horizon

Employees use information in differing ways within an organization, often depending on their role. Variations of complexity of experience of IL can mirror variation in workplace role and the corresponding complexity of knowledge needed on a day-to-day basis to fulfil that role. Senior roles, involving strategic thinking, involve very complex information experiences in comparison to those employees whose horizons are comparatively limited. Of course, work activity is seldom this distinct. In 'short-term' activities dealing with immediate information need the individual may operate outside a level of Information Literacy complexity associated with their role. Sometimes senior figures have simpler experiences and more junior ones more complex – especially if the latter are involved in group or teamwork which may have a complex aim. Bruce (1997) made it clear that any individual may experience IL at any level of sophistication, depending on context.

Therefore in terms of the workplace, variation in complexity in IL experience is of two types:

1   The immediate context – an individual's IL experience has a complexity determined by a knowledge need in a particular immediate workplace activity or situation.
2   The role context – a professional's IL experience is affected by their job or role within the wider organization. This is their usual IL 'horizon'. Strategically focused senior managers usually have more complex exper- iences then those operating at less complex levels of knowledge need.

The whole range of levels of complexity of IL experience as described by all of the Categories of Description from a research study such as described in Chapter 2 are relevant, to some extent, to the experiences of the workforce as a whole. More senior figures are able to operate at all levels of complexity and have an information horizon which is panoramic while still focused on detail.

Although individuals often operate at other, usually lower, levels of complexity of Information Literacy experience, their usual role-focused level is their principal horizon, one which reflects the way they see their information world. What do such information horizons look like and how can they be described? As shown in Chapter 2, Categories of Description can be developed by bringing together dimensions of a similar complexity from each of the several Themes of Expanding Awareness. It is possible, through careful analysis of the contextual experiences described by each dimension from each theme and how they apparently interrelate, to give each category a detailed description characterizing that workplace information horizon corresponding to the experience of IL at that particular level of complexity. A diagram showing these relationships was given in Figure 2.1.

The six categories in the nursing study (Forster, 2015a) and the description of their associated information horizons are given below. There is nothing to suggest that the levels of complexity of experience of IL described in these categories are not equivalent to those in other professions and workplaces; that the nature of the knowledge developed associated with similar experiences in other professions and workplaces does not facilitate similar professional roles:

A **The passive minimalist.** This nurse obtains 'the facts' to deal with the immediate and simple issue or context. Passive information absorption occurs as frequently as information gathering; the latter may frequently be of the 'scavenging' type.

B **The knowledgeable goal achiever.** This way of experiencing IL is one in which the nurse is focused on specific goals. Information is sought out, identified and applied in the context of specific clinical requirements; this is done in conjunction with a developing background knowledge which allows the nurse to know how to address these aims. Skills and relationships are developed with such goals in mind.

C **The focused, competent and evolving professional.** In this information horizon IL is usually experienced as processes of professional effectiveness and achieved functionality. This is governed by a widening awareness of the value of finding and applying evidence and other information sources and the ability to do so in terms of what can be achieved in improved practice and patient outcome.

D **The confident and trusted promoter of justifiable change.** In this information horizon IL is experienced as a means to, and stimulus for, an incipient tendency to think abstractly and strategically and as a leader. Such a nurse is transforming him/herself into someone confident, trusted and with that increasing grasp of the parameters of practice which results in an understanding of the potential value of change and where and how it may usefully occur.

E   **The teacher and promoter of an evidence-based culture.** In this information horizon IL is experienced in transformative contributions to roles which are expanding in horizon and in which a wider strategic focus is beginning to operate. Evidence is skilfully obtained and applied towards the development of policy. A leading contribution is made to the development of an information-rich culture, often in a teaching role, especially with junior staff.

F   **The leader, philosopher and strategist.** The most sophisticated level of experience of IL operates in the context of the nurse as leader, through its part in the promotion of the development of the ability to think strategically and philosophically. The ethics of obtaining or failing to obtain the evidence for best practice, the relationship of evidence to knowledge and experience and the strategic use of evidence and other information are amongst the challenging contexts in which IL is experienced.

Librarians and educators are challenged to recognize this variation within a profession's information world and to adapt IL education and development initiatives accordingly. Information sources, IL and knowledge development needs may be variable in nature, complexity and purpose. A librarian, when supporting professionals and students training for workplace roles, must bear in mind that sensitivity to these factors is essential in both enquiry work and IL training. Professionals operate at different levels of complexity of information need and knowledge development contexts and librarian responses should reflect this. What is the information horizon of the worker? How might she or he populate, fulfil and develop the dimensions of that horizon? How might an educator lead a student in the professions to understand that profession's range of 'Information horizons'?

Information Literacy relationships: teamwork and empowerment

A key aspect of the 'personal' dimension of IL experience is the development and maintenance, through information exchange and collaborative knowledge development, of working relationships within the team, department and organization, and beyond this with clients or patients. The former often involves the mutual development of knowledge of group, organizational or business value (Lloyd, 2010; Williams, Cooper and Wavell, 2014; Forster, 2015a). This 'collaborative Information Literacy' has its own processes and information forms, as researchers such as Lloyd (2006; 2010) and Inskip (2014) have found:

There is a greater emphasis on people (as opposed to texts) as information sources; thus, developing an understanding of workplace IL practice means appreciating the social and informal ways in which information is processed into knowledge.

Goldstein and Whitworth, 2014, 1

Modern workplaces worldwide operate in increasingly complex ways (Ouye, 2011). To continue to be efficient in achieving the organization's aims they must deal with increasingly complex information, which is often multi-sourced and multidisciplinary (Skyrius and Bujauskas, 2010). It follows that information-literate individuals often need to work in teams in order to cope with the knowledge demands of contemporary working life, demands that are not only overwhelming but complex, often involving a range of sources of varying 'subject' or professional provenance. An information-literate individual in the workplace must operate through 'information relationships' of collaboration and sharing.

As is highlighted by other contributors to this book and elsewhere, the key characteristic of IL in the workplace is its sociological–contextual–collaborative dimension of focus; a perspective often neglected or misunderstood by librarians. It 'manifests in the process of learning about the sociality of the workplace as an intersubjective space; and enables the development of practical understandings about performance at work' (Lloyd, 2010, 89), and exhibits a 'focus on collaboration, teamwork and development of shared understanding about practice and performance' (Lloyd, 2010, 103) through a shared socio-cultural understanding of what counts as information and information need, a grasp of the contextual nature of that need and a group-focused interpretation of information's significance and value in that context. Information need may in itself be shared or may be recognized by a single person within the team or partnership; the processes of formulating the scope and range of an information search, the critiquing of the information gathered and its management and presentation, might be undertaken by one or more of the team; but the knowledge to be developed to fulfil its wider function within a workplace organization is the focus of the team's purpose and function as a whole. That information can be documentary, but not necessarily (Lupton, 2004; 2008). Lloyd (2006), for example, found that the range of information types used by firefighters included a mutual information exchange which often had a physical and sensory dimension important in the maintenance of a functional team.

Hepworth and Smith (2008), in a study of support staff in a university, identified a strong collaborative and contextual dimension; IL was a matter of teamwork operating in those roles set out for the team by the wider organization. Some research has suggested IL, when experienced in health settings (O'Farrill, 2008; Forster, 2015a), is also frequently collaborative, either between professionals (the multidisciplinary team) or between professionals and their patients or patients' families; each relationship operating under shared socio-cultural parameters of practice, and recognized contexts of care and need:

> The roles of seeker and provider [of information] are not static. For example during a medical examination, a doctor can be a provider then a seeker, or both simultaneously.
>
> Lombard, 2010, 2

The nursing study strongly emphasized the importance of that 'multidisciplinary team' in the use of information in clinical practice, as well as the value of 'clinical guidelines' developed by teams of specialists who analyse the research literature to produce guidance to fellow professionals. Information use appears to be part of the fabric of teamworking and therefore the development and maintenance of teams. Information Literacy can be seen as 'encouraging dialogue . . . through initiation of purposeful sense-making and knowledge creation opportunities' (Bruce, Hughes and Somerville, 2012, 18).

How might a 'collaborative' experience of IL show itself in terms of workplace activity? How does IL work within a team and the individual make his or her personal contribution? What are the dynamics by which knowledge is developed by and for the team and wider organization through effective information use? How does IL drive and facilitate the day-to-day operation of a team or organization so that it fulfils its function and wider purpose and that of the individual professional? These questions are only beginning to be answered.

Teams operate through the exchange of information and knowledge (Hatala and Lutta, 2009). One must understand one's role, what one contributes to the team, what others contribute and what the team seeks to achieve. All of this involves the exchange of information. The result is mutual trust and understanding (Lombard, 2010), a sense of achievement and being appreciated and valued – all achieved through a dynamic of mutual IL experience.

Bruce, Hughes and Somerville (2012); Hepworth and Smith (2008); Mirijamdotter (2010); Lloyd (2006; 2010); Partridge, Edwards and Thorpe (2010) and Forster (2015a), and others, suggest IL is intrinsic to personal effectiveness within a team or organizational context by contributing to increasing information flow, by facilitating information location and application, which leads to a greater understanding of the organization's, the team's and one's own knowledge base. This can facilitate decision-making abilities beyond the immediate sphere through a more creative use of knowledge. The individual develops a deeper sense of responsibility for the team outcome. Each individual feels an increased sense of 'making a difference' within the organization and team through an improved understanding of the organizational purpose.

In the nursing study, a theme within IL experience which explicitly described such a collaborative dimension was: *IL experienced in development and maintenance of relationships with patients, patients' families, colleagues and other professionals.* Information sharing and knowledge development collaboration was not only experienced within the team but between the professional and patients and their families. The theme had the following range of dimensions of experience ranging from the least to the most complex:

A. Interacting passively with others – others as a source of information:
    - receiving information from patients, colleagues and other professionals.
B. Interacting actively – a give and take of information:
    - sharing information with patients, colleagues and other professionals.
C. Developing functional relationships:
    - functioning as part of the multidisciplinary team.
D. Developing the trust of patients, families and colleagues:
    - creating trust in you in others
    - being seen to be accountable for actions
    - achieving autonomy and status within the team.
E. Developing a teaching role:
    - functioning as a teacher for junior colleagues and other members of the team.
F. Developing a leadership role:
    - becoming a patient advocate
    - fulfilling a leadership role within the team.

As experience of IL in this theme expands and deepens in complexity, it promotes the development of relationships from non-mutual to mutual interactions, which when further enriched and stabilized become 'trust'. A further expansion of the complexity of IL experience enables the nurse to take on a teaching role in relation to fellow nurses, and with greater complexity, a leadership role (interpreted as a teaching role of greater depth, breadth and complexity). IL is experienced as a tool and impetus in the achievement of these roles. Hence, collaboration is passive or active, narrowly focused or 'strategic', depending on the level of complexity of experience and the level of exploitation of the potentialities of IL's ability to develop complex knowledge for the partnership, team or organization.

Information Literacy as a conduit of intimacy, empowerment and trust

As can be seen in the findings above, Information Literacy-powered relationships extend beyond colleagues to clients, patients and their families. Information is power, and the empowerment of those vulnerable groups that look to professionals to guide and heal them is an important role for many professionals. Chapter 7 looks at how professionals have an ethical obligation to be information-literate in order to be fully informed about key facts and research evidence, lack of knowledge of which may affect the quality of their service or performance. This obligation also applies in a slightly different context, one in which IL is a source of that correct and complete information about their medical, legal or other personal problem which might give patients and clients reassurance and autonomy. This flow of complete and reliable information helps establish a relationship between the professional and their client, customer or patient which is empowering and/or reassuring in itself. This relationship may well result in the client, patient or family member feeling more comfortable in sharing certain types of information that they may not have been in a more formal context.

Information Literacy's role in professional and career development

As described above and elsewhere, research studies have shown that the experience of IL is focused on knowledge development and learning (Forster, 2015c). The 'meaning' of such experience is located in the nature of the knowledge developed through information location and critique. Knowledge, and the ability to develop knowledge, can be applied in a workplace environment, through effective performance of one's role not only for the benefit of the team and organization, but also for personal professional development.

How do we develop in our professional lives? Both training and experience allow us to increase our competence and understanding; the former in large, perhaps not always contextual, leaps, the latter slowly and perhaps not always soundly. However, the ability to identify a knowledge gap and to find, use and apply appropriate information to fill it gives an individual an autonomous learning dynamic which potentially corrects misinterpreted experiences, reinforces and contextualizes training and opens further horizons. Above all, information use is a part of the professional's day-to-day engagement with the workplace; learning is continually focused on immediate professional need, while at the same time always nudging beyond the current horizon.

There was one theme in the nursing study which described dimensions of IL experience which showed this 'bumping up' against professional horizons

– a theme which suggests, by its very existence, that IL in the workplace has a self-developmental aspect: *Information Literacy experienced in processes of professional self-development*. Again, with a range of experiences from least complex (A) to the most complex (F):

A. Seeking out knowledge of clinical contexts and conditions:
   • investigate newly encountered clinical conditions/situations.
B. Being a knowledgeable nurse:
   • establishing knowledge of, and understanding of, current practice and associated issues.
C. Achieving professional competence:
   • showing competence in day-to-day work.
D. Achieving professional confidence:
   • feeling confident in one's role
   • progressing professionally; becoming a lifelong learner.
E. Achieving functional autonomy:
   • becoming an adaptable, flexible and responsive professional
   • becoming able to function non-dependently within the team.
F. Having the ability to think and behave strategically:
   • becoming innovative and developmental in practice
   • developing a wider, strategic professional horizon.

IL experiences here are at their simplest when they involve the effective seeking out of knowledge of specific conditions to enable a basic professional functionality. More complex experiences contribute to a sense of 'being knowledgeable': working towards day-to-day effectiveness in the job. Still more complex IL experience contributes to the more complex state of 'competence' which involves the ability to determine and develop all relevant knowledge needed for the performance of the designated role. A still greater complexity of experience leads to a sense of 'confidence', facilitating an interest in wider horizons and a developing self-direction: a mid-stage between competence and autonomy. The higher level of 'autonomy' might allow the individual to take on basic training and mentorship roles, with a new contextual understanding of the professional role: seeing it from 'outside'. The highest level of IL experience is one in which the individual is able to bring to bear, within a senior role, a broad, strategic perspective and innovative style.

Again, there is no reason why this should not be a model for IL experience in other workplaces than the medical. IL education which develops the capacity for more complex information experiences is key here. The individual can, often using formal training as a base, apply an increase in personal knowledge, and an improving capacity to develop more complex knowledge, in order to progress continually to higher levels of workplace functionality. The individual experiences IL in the context of the fulfilment of a particular role in the workplace, but IL can also be experienced as part of a developing interest in, understanding of and capacity for a higher role. An individual, through learning processes (Bruce and Hughes, 2010) themselves initiated through IL's knowledge development function, begins to develop that capacity for wider, and more *complex*, responsibility.

Conclusion

Librarians, library managers and academics have the task of emphasizing the role of IL in the human dimension of personal horizon, connectivity, personal growth and sensitivity to the needs of others, within the professions and workplace. Managers and team leaders must also take in the implications that without IL a team will fail to function, not only through failures in the dynamics of information sharing and knowledge development vital to an organization's well-being and the inability of individuals to experience the information horizon appropriate for their roles, but though a brittleness and insensitivity towards customers, clients or patients. IL and IL education are profoundly integral to a perceptive and vibrant organization.

CHAPTER 4

From transaction to transformation: organizational learning and knowledge creation experience within Informed Systems

Mary M. Somerville and Christine S. Bruce

This chapter will discuss:

- an organizational approach known as Informed Systems, which builds learning conditions and knowledge creation experiences that result in a workplace which uses information effectively to learn, adapt and perform.

Introduction

This chapter describers the Informed Systems approach to building organizational learning conditions and knowledge creation experiences through effective workplace communication systems and information practices. Informed Systems, which has its roots in relational Information Literacy (IL) (see Chapter 2), integrates constructivist learning, systems thinking and knowledge creation theories to advance 'Informed Learning', the experience of using information to learn, within constructed workplace ecosystems. Activated as action research and enacted through participatory co-design, this approach focuses on collective inquiry to further learning relationships and Informed Learning experiences (i.e. advances both information and learning experiences simultaneously). Associated professional practices facilitated by both technology- and human-enabled workplace communication systems guide the experience of using information to learn. Such experiences are amplified by dialogue and reflection, to foster knowledge creation for 'learning in action'. Central to the Informed Systems approach is nimble thought leadership and collaborative information-focused activities, customizable to changing local situations that foster Informed Learning capacity in the contemporary workplace.

In this chapter, workplace IL is understood to be the experience of using information to learn, in the tradition of the relational approach to IL. In *The Seven Faces of Information Literacy* and *Informed Learning*, Bruce (1997; 2008) presents insights into the experience of using information to learn through a relational approach. The early research results include four principles integral to the relational view and seven faces (facets or categories) representing qualitatively different ways of experiencing the use of information to learn. In depicting the phenomenon as a whole, these principles and categories represent an integration of experiential, contextual and transformational information experiences, which departed from the predominant behavioural research and skills-based education in vogue when she released her findings.

The relational approach recognizes these guiding elements, based on Paul Ramsden's (1988, 26) principles associated with a phenomenographic approach to learning, for using information to learn (adapted from Bruce, 1997, 174):

- Learning to use information to learn is about changes in conception – that is, developing new, more complex ways of conceiving of, or experiencing, information and information use.
- Learning to use information to learn always has content as well as process – that is, people should be learning about something (e.g. disciplinary content) as they engage in learning to be effective information users.
- Learning to use information to learn is about relations between the learner and the subject matter – that is, learning to be an effective information user involves the relations between the learner and information.
- Improving the experience of using information to learn is about understanding the learner's perspective – that is, helping people to become better information users requires understanding their ways of experiencing effective information use.

Within this guiding framework, which simultaneously focuses on information use and learning, the qualitatively different ways of experiencing using information to learn, adapted for workplace contexts and listed below (adapted from Bruce, Hughes and Somerville, 2012), should be understood as suggesting a relationship between information and its contexts of use, including what information is used for.

1   Information and communication technologies: harnessing technology for information awareness, communication and management.
2   Information sources: using information sources (including people) for workplace learning and action taking.
3   Information and knowledge generation processes: developing personal

practices or heuristics for finding and using information for novel situations.

4 Information curation and knowledge management: organizing and managing data, information and knowledge for future professional needs.

5 Knowledge construction and worldview transformation: building knowledge through discovery, evaluation, discernment and application.

6 Collegial sharing and knowledge extension: exercising and extending professional practices and knowledge bases to workplace insights.

7 Professional wisdom and workplace learning: contributing to collegial learning through using information to learn to take better action to improve.

Taken together, the categories represent the experience of Informed Learning, 'the phenomenon as a whole' (Bruce, 1997, 38), within which learning is understood as changes in how the phenomenon is experienced. Thus, in workplaces or workspaces, learning to fully realize the potential of information experiences requires developing the full range of ways of experiencing the multifaceted phenomenon.

When professionals become aware of how they experience using information to learn within a context, they become more effective within those contexts as they learn what it takes to make that possible. Within the workplace, for instance, awareness can be furthered through reflective engagement guided by learning-centred information practices – a process of subjective knowledge development leading to increased understanding that transforms transactions to transformations (Somerville, 2015b).

The evolution of Informed Systems

Since 2003, Informed Systems has evolved both through and as a process of organizational design for learning in action, with the intention of fostering information exchange, reflective dialogue, knowledge creation and conceptual change. Results from evaluative studies (e.g. Somerville, Schader and Huston, 2005; Somerville et al., 2007; Somerville, 2009; Somerville and Howard, 2010; Mirijamdotter and Somerville, 2009; Somerville, 2015a) reveal that, over time and with practice, this collaborative learning approach increases co-workers' capacity for creating systems and producing knowledge.

Critical features of the approach include that it is activated by participatory design and action research, amplified by systems thinking and rooted in Informed Learning (Somerville, 2015a). In 'working together' (Somerville, 2009) to generate knowledge, colleagues contribute complementary knowledge skills, work responsibilities and social perspectives which advance social, relational and interactive aspects of work life (Townsend, 2014). Organizational capacity builds as colleagues engage in using information to learn in ever-expanding professional contexts that exercise evidence-based decision making and action taking (Somerville and Chatzipanagiotou, 2015).

It naturally follows that for this approach to 'travel' – i.e. to prove transferable to other settings – the design of decision-making processes occurs within a larger consideration of organizational structure and workplace culture, which requires local clarification of elements of process design and professional practice appropriate within those circumstances for making collaborative informed decisions. This includes fostering a culture in which information is honoured, processes are transparent and learning is valued. In addition, organizational values and practices must appreciate knowledge generation and therefore support routine collection of local data, organized for discovery, access and use in future decision making, enacted as evidence-based decision making (Somerville and Kloda, 2016).

Learning the way to change: from theory to practice

Between 2003 and 2015, research-in-practice studies based on participatory design and action learning evolved this integrated Informed Systems approach to encourage persistent workplace inquiry within North American university libraries. Three theories, elaborated below, were adapted and integrated to enable robust organizational learning. The work of theorists Christine S. Bruce from Australia (who advanced Informed Learning) and Peter Checkland from England (who developed soft systems methodology) promotes the kind of learning made possible through evolving and transferable capacity to use information to learn within collaboratively designed workplace communication systems with associated professional practices. Over this period, workplace evolution involved initiating systems co-design activities to stimulate participants' appreciation of the potential relational understandings of effective information use (Checkland and Holwell, 1998; Bruce 1997). Then co-designed socio-cultural practices strategically continued workplace learning, implementing Christine S. Bruce's *Informed Learning* (Bruce, 2008), and, more recently, information experiences (Bruce et al., 2014).

The emergent Informed Systems approach recognizes the organization as a knowledge ecosystem consisting of a complex set of interactions between people, process, technology and content. Within this context, knowledge emerges through individuals' exchange of resources, ideas and experiences (Nonaka, 1994). It naturally follows that:

knowledge-related work requires thinking – not only monitoring, browsing, searching, selecting, finding, recognizing, sifting, sorting and manipulating but also being creative, always questioning, interpreting, understanding situations, adapting to changes, tailoring, handling data created, e.g., in the lab, with particular focus on how to put questions, draw inferences, give explanations and conclusions, prioritize . . . within complex, ever-changing environments.

Materska, 2013, 231

In response, Informed Systems evolved to foster information exchange, reflective dialogue, knowledge creation and conceptual change within organizations. Over time and with practice, this approach progressed co-workers' capacity for creating knowledge creation systems through engagement in participatory design, amplified by systems thinking and exercised by collective discourse. Colleagues with differing but complementary knowledge skills and work responsibilities advanced social, relational and interactive aspects of work life through which transferable learning occurs and organizational capacity builds (Somerville, 2015b). More specifically, systemic leadership and collaboration models promoted collective 'sense making' that guides organizational 'action taking' (Somerville, 2015a). Collective knowledge creation capabilities are exercised and extended as continuous improvements develop through workplace systems, relationships and practices that support continuous learning and refine local practices.

Learning the way: through action to improve

External evaluation of Informed Systems outcomes at California Polytechnic State University from 2003 to 2006 and at the University of Colorado Denver from 2008 to 2015 demonstrate the efficacy of cultivating Informed Learning experiences within enabling, co-designed workplace systems. Results in California and Colorado revealed the synergy of systems perspectives and knowledge practices that – in combination – aim to further organizational learning. From the beginning, research results suggested that (Somerville, Schader and Huston, 2005, 222–3):

- Integral to the creation of a robust learning organization, leaders are responsible for design of workplace environments supportive of information-rich conversations.
- Systems thinking can be used to contextualize workplace issues in terms that revisit both the nature of organizational information and the purpose of organizational work.
- It follows that as leaders apply systems thinking methodologies and tools to understand the complexities of the organization and its

situation, staff members learn to diagnose problems, identify consequences and make informed responses within a holistic context.

Longitudinal research findings corroborate that application of these principles changes how co-workers think and what they think about the phenomenon of workplace learning – i.e. the *what* and *how* of their learning (Somerville, 2015a):

- More specifically, people come to see the underlying context and assumptions for their decisions. This new relational understanding predisposes them to adjust their assumptions and strategies as they learn – in other words, as they change their awareness or experience of their appreciative settings.
- Over time and with practice, as people adopt systems and design thinking and tools, collective capacity grows. Successful responses to new information and unique situations evolve as collective awareness of organizational potential grows.
- And, finally, sustained conversations rich in relational context ensure substantial content for transforming the organizational culture. Enabled by maturing collective awareness, dialogue assumes creative potential as it activates rethinking and transformative learning.

The elements of Informed Systems

The Informed Systems approach offers an information-focused and systems-enabled approach for 'working together' (Somerville, 2009) in contemporary learning organizations to develop more effective professional and workplace information use. Within the larger framework of the contemporary knowledge ecosystem, Informed Learning is positioned at the nexus of information experience, technology experience and learning experience (Somerville, 2015a), essential learning elements embodied in the holistic Informed Systems transformation approach.

Then, with a focus on inquiry- and evidence-based activities to make decisions and take actions within an enabling learning environment, the Informed Systems approach guides co-workers to identify the decisions to be made and the information to be considered for those decisions (Somerville, 2015a). The leadership model guides thought processes for co-creation of organizational learning conditions requisite for collegial inquiry. Then, at a more operational level, the information process model advances problematizing of the situation, to coalesce shared understanding of inquiry aims, as well as iterative review for continuous local improvements and transferable learning capabilities. This is accomplished through collaborative design and iterative evaluation (Somerville et al., 2007) of workplace systems, relationships, and practices. Over time, increasingly effective, efficient and elegant organizational structures and professional processes both facilitate renewal and increase responsiveness (Somerville, 2015a; Somerville and Chatzipanagiotou, 2015). Practical outcomes have included user interface customization (Somerville, 2013), technical services reorganization (Pan and Howard, 2009), participatory facility redesign (Somerville and Brown-Sica, 2011), and organizational culture revitalization (Pan and Howard, 2010; Somerville and Farner, 2012), which illustrate the transferability of Informed Systems to a variety of workplace learning situations.

This catalytic approach anticipates that fundamental transformation in workplace culture requires that co-workers design and enact information-focused and evidence-based learning experiences. They thereby learn the way to decision making and action taking. Increasingly more complex experiences of information exchange, sense making and knowledge creation, well supported by workplace communication systems and professional information practices, promote dialogue and reflection and thereby enrich analysis and interpretation of complexities and interdependencies (Somerville, 2015a; Somerville and Chatzipanagiotou, 2015).

Learning the way: continuous workplace learning

Enactment of workplace learning requires an enabling environment for information exchange, sense making and knowledge creation activities that advance information use and learning relationships among 'resilient workers' (Lloyd, 2013). 'Within such a "whole systems" framework, organizational leadership must establish and embed . . . sustainable social interactions and enabling workplace systems' (Somerville, 2015a, 49) that can successfully determine: 'What information . . . experiences do we want to facilitate or make possible? What information and learning experiences are vital to further our . . . professional work?' (Bruce, 2013, 20). Such perspectives encourage consideration of provocative questions, such as:

> What constitutes information? What informed learning experiences are being used? What information experiences appear? What is being learned? How is understanding/experience of the world changing? What can we do to enrich informed learning experiences? . . . to introduce new experiences? How would access to a range of experiences, and awareness of these experiences, be demonstrated?
>
> Bruce, 2012

Intentional organizational learning is thereby enriched through an information experience lens, whereby participants collectively expand their learning horizons through engaging within co-designed communication systems and associated sharing processes. As depicted in Informed Systems models, requisite information-sharing relationships extend beyond traditional team boundaries because knowledge creation requires holistic appreciation of the interrelated elements of workplace information experience which include: its situatedness; its connection with Informed Learning and informed decisions; and its cognitive and social dimensions, through critical and creative information use that produces generation and sharing of new knowledge useful in taking purposeful action (Somerville and Mirijamdotter, 2014). In response, Informed Systems (re)learning models, conducted within enabling systems infrastructure, further collaborative professional processes that are learning-focused and information intensive, to promote sense making and enable workplace learning. Therefore, within an Informed Systems framework, action-oriented inquiry is paired with inclusive decision making fortified by inquiry-based dialogue and information-centred reflection.

Informed Systems outcomes

Since 2003, practical workplace outcomes have confirmed the efficacy of an Informed Systems approach to organizational learning. As collective appreciation has grown for an education, rather than a service, focus, a consultative (learning) mindset replaced earlier transactional ('busyness') priorities. Concurrently, collective conceptions shifted from 'library as warehouse' to 'library as learning space' and 'systems thinking' replaced 'silo thinking' (Somerville and Farner, 2012; Somerville, 2015a). These outcomes recognize that, because organizational culture is experienced as a shared basis of appreciation and action (Schön, 1983), it can be transformed through persistent communication sustained by intentional learning relationships.

Learning the way: workplace learning synergies

For organizational learning to occur, information encounters must be experienced as sufficiently contextualized to activate and extend prior under-standing (Bruce, 1997). When the workplace is conceptualized in this way,

> people can learn to create knowledge on the basis of their concrete experiences, through observing and reflecting on that experience, by forming abstract concepts and generalizations, and by testing the implications of these concepts in new situations, which lead to new concrete experience that initiates a new cycle. This assertion fortified our aspiration to develop reflective practitioners who

learn through critical (and self-critical) collaborative inquiry processes that foster individual self-evaluation, collective problem-formulation, inclusive contextualized inquiry, and professional development.

Somerville and Mirijamdotter, 2014, 206

In 'learning the way' to workplace synergies, Informed Learning serves as a theoretical construct that encourages exploration of learning-related aspects of information experience, here defined as 'contextualized instances of using information. It integrates all information-related actions, thoughts, feelings, and has social and cultural dimensions.' (Hughes, 2014, 34). Informed Learning provides a pedagogical framework, which encourages expansion of learners' information using and learning experiences. In other words, Informed Learning enables making increased sense of multiple information experiences through intentional expansion of information engagements. As colleagues initiate and sustain inquiries and design actions which are information-centred, action-oriented and learning-enabled, their professional experiences transform. They reinvent roles, responsibilities, processes and relationships as active collaborators in the process and co-design their future.

Compelling questions shift as organizational focus shifts. This occurs organically when members of contemporary organizations create information-rich learning environments within teams and people learn to co-create knowledge-enabling systemic structures and processes for 'knowing' relevant information landscapes. Co-designed learning activities generate and sustain workplace synergies for knowledge creation and social interaction. New relationships encourage sharing of information, skills, expertise and experience exchanged through co-designed practices that further repurposing, redirecting, reorganizing and relearning for forward movement and nimble responsiveness. Simultaneously, the co-created communication systems and socialization practices produce increasing variation and complexity in information experiences.

Over time and with practice, these processes and activities transform organizational culture. Reactive and conservative impulses are transformed to proactive and generative responses. In increasingly vibrant learning environments, knowledge emerges through encounters that transform understanding within individuals and among groups. Such

practice of organizational learning involves developing tangible activities: new governing ideas, innovation in infrastructure, and new management methods and tools for changing the way people conduct their work. Given the opportunity to take part in these new activities, people will develop an enduring capacity for change . . . with far greater levels of diversity, commitment, innovation and talent.

Senge, 1999, 33

In addition,

> people will continually expand their capacity to create the results they truly desire, where new and expansive patterns of thinking are nurtured, where collective aspiration is set free, and where people are continually learning how to learn together.
>
> Senge, 1990, 3

Systemic aims: organizational transformation

A practical example within the Technical Services Department at the University of Colorado Denver Library illustrates the efficacy of integrating information, technology and learning elements to promote using information to learn, as explicated through organizational capacity-building categories revealed in *Informed Learning* (Bruce, 2008).

1 Information and Communication Technology evaluation and design: in 2008, technical services staff members implemented a commercial electronic resources management (ERM) system to manage data about academic e-resources acquisitions, licensing, troubleshooting and usage statistics. Sadly, this incident involved incorrect product selection and inadequate vendor communications – reflecting the state of organizational decision making at that time.

In 2009, participatory design of technology-enabled communication systems and associated professional information practices commenced (Mirijamdotter, 2015, 151–63). Teams employed an iterative learning process (Checkland and Poulter, 2006) to clarify the purpose(s) of internal communication systems. They then began a selection process for a new ERM system, keenly aware of the importance of defining system software outcomes in the request for proposals. In this way, staff members began to develop new capacity to evaluate and design technology-enabled systems and associated human workflows.

2 Information sources identification and evaluation: despite the improved ERM system, e-resources database management continued to require considerable troubleshooting, due to the many reasons that disrupt service. These could include lapsed database subscriptions or incorrect Internet Protocol (IP) addresses, university network outages, vendor maintenance downtime and user account issues.

So from 2009 onward, technical services staff developed increased familiarity with potentially relevant data and information sources. They learned that effectively managed information facilitates collaboration and advances organizational learning and decision making (Pan, Bradbeer and Jurries, 2011). While exploration often began with peer-reviewed publications, authoritative evidence also included other information sources and professional knowledge: quantitative and qualitative research results, local statistics, open access data, and even accumulated knowledge, opinion, relationships and instinct were used, depending on local circumstances. Team members became increasingly able to consider what forms of evidence contribute to decisions, to weigh that evidence and to make transparent decisions, within complex workplace contexts.

3   Information exchange and knowledge generation: in response to a wide variety of potential problems and possible data, staff members frequently exchanged e-mails to resolve problems, supplemented by regular in-person meetings. Although valuable knowledge was exchanged, participants recognized that these processes did not centralize information about tracking status or problem trends. Data remained data; it was not yet able to inform (Browning, 2015).
4   Knowledge curation and management capabilities: in response, three troubleshooting librarians began to experiment with customizing software to prevent problems from being lost or forgotten and to record and prioritize reported incidents. Their evolving systems and improved workflows facilitated documentation so that effective steps to solving problems could be retrieved at a later date (Pan and Howard, 2009; Browning, 2016).
5   Professional practices and workplace learning: over time, the troubleshooting team recognized that vast amounts of data about access issues were being collected in problem reports. Team members decided to analyse the data. Results revealed that electronic access issues involve many entities, systems and resources, requiring cross-department collaboration. Complex problems required persistent monitoring and repeated examination, necessitating refinement of workflows, initiation of new collaborations (Browning, 2015; 2016), and hiring of additional staff.

Over the years, Technical Services members became designers of systems and practices for collaborative evidence-based decision making. Transformative Informed Systems models guided well contextualized, information-rich conversations wherein inter-professional co-workers revisited both the nature of organizational information and the purpose of organizational work. This workplace knowledge development is focused on the team's and organization's aims and priorities. It is experienced in, and transferable to, a range of contexts and settings and is fundamental to the learning process as a transformative generator of knowledge.

Informed Systems transferability

> Academic environments are seeing rapid change in their intellectual,
> technological and economic directions. Consequently, libraries must keep abreast
> of emerging issues and evolving demands, engage with their changing
> communities, innovate in the face of resource constraints, and communicate their
> actions and intentions clearly.
>
> Loo and Dupois, 2015, 671

Such heightened expectations place considerable pressure on academic librarians to fulfil current needs and anticipate future opportunities. These expectations and priorities are significant in many other workplaces, due to similar external pressures and environmental developments.

Informed Systems is well suited to furthering workplace renewal, including redesigning facilities, reconsidering collections and reinventing services, because it conceptualizes the organization as a learning entity. The approach recognizes the inadequacy of reliance on 'busyness' statistics, such as gate counts and article downloads, as accountability measures (Somerville and Chatzipanagiotou, 2015, 3). Rather,

> systemic changes require systemic responses because a case-by-case or incident-
> by-incident response was inadequate, given the magnitude of transformation
> underway. In response, Informed Systems – which integrates complementary
> information- and learning-focused theories – addresses a research-in-practice
> problem that emerges from a problem of practice – i.e., the lack of an integrated
> model to inform workplace learning in contemporary information and
> knowledge organizations.
>
> Somerville, 2015a, 45

Informed Systems principles and practices exercise and enable participatory design, action learning and perpetual inquiry to catalyse constituent engagement, create shared vision, and build stakeholder partnerships through using information to learn. Systemic activity and process models activate collaborative evidence-based information processes within enabling conditions for thought leadership and workplace learning. Persistent cultivation of rich information experiences through information-centred and action-oriented dialogue and reflection advances information exchange and knowledge creation, through which transferable learning occurs and organizational capacity builds (Somerville et al., 2014). Thought leadership and collaborative practice guide – and are guided by – participatory design and knowledge creation.

Throughout, organizational decision making and action taking requires leadership oversight of interactions between new knowledge and shifting contexts (Mirijamdotter, 2010; Somerville and Chatzipanagiotou, 2015), supported by workplace practices that move collective thinking forward. 'Knowledge and understanding are thereby learned through the active function of practice by an individual, within the larger body of practice' (Koufogiannakis, 2013, 166). Reflective practitioners learn through community experiences within workplace ecosystems in which intersubjectively created meaning is reinforced and changes over time through constant negotiation (Gherardi, 2009a) of complexities and interdependencies.

Informed Systems transformation: essential workplace elements

Informed Systems recognizes that individuals select information from the workplace (and extended) environment based upon a worldview consisting of existing interests, experience and values. Within this systemic context, thought leaders and knowledge activists offer filters to select what is important from available information models to expand individuals' ability to understand and use information to learn (Nonaka, 1994). These interventions are challenging because tacit knowledge 'consists of mental models, beliefs, and perspectives so ingrained that we take them for granted and therefore cannot easily articulate them' (Nonaka, 2007, 165). However, as 'new explicit knowledge is shared throughout an organization, other employees begin to internalize it – that is, they use it to broaden, extend, and reframe their own tacit knowledge' (Nonaka, 2007, 166) through 'purposeful discourse focused on exploring, constructing meaning and validating understanding' (Garrison, 2014, 147).

In practice, Informed Systems requires the design of enabling systems and informing activities through a strong 'people-oriented' approach, customizable to local circumstances. The approach recognizes that workplace learning originates from interactions and relationships among organizational members, which enable investigation and negotiation of diverse interests, judgements and decisions. Reflection and dialogue processes promote learning through critical (and self-critical) inquiry experiences that foster individual self-evaluation, collective problem formulation and nuanced professional development (Somerville and Mirijamdotter, 2014). Informed Systems thereby promotes transformation in organizational awareness and workplace behaviour through intentional design that nurtures engagement among individuals and with information.

Organizational readiness factors

Informed Systems employs organizational design principles and professional information practices that enable and enact collaborative decision making and action taking within an inquiry-intensive and evidence-based workplace attentive to both process and content. In a workplace culture in which collective processes are transparent and evidence sources are privileged over speculation or opinion, purposeful learning processes are necessarily collegial, conducted within a positive work environment, enabled by appropriate processes for open discussions for decision making and action taking. 'Knowledge and understanding are thereby learned through active . . . practice by an individual, within the larger body of practice' (Schön, 1983, 50), which situates and contextualizes intersubjectively created meaning. Understanding changes over time through renegotiation.

Enactment of workplace learning requires an enabling environment for information-exchange, sense-making and knowledge creation activities that advance information use and learning relationships through socio-cultural processes and practices co-designed by co-workers. Collective capacity for discussion and analysis of complexities and interdependencies grows through intentional construction and reconstruction of the learner during interactive relationships and sustainable networks comprised of information, technology and people. Such 'construction of learning, of learners and of the environments in which they operate' (Hager, 2004, 12) evolve to adopt and adapt, create and recreate, contextualize and recontextualize through wider and wider circles of consultation, co-operation and collaboration. Requisite workplace conditions must necessarily, therefore, also account for the human interactions and organizational complexity within which decisions are being made.

Despite considerable organizational variation, some 'lessons learned' have emerged about conditions that foster workplace learning (Somerville and Kloda, 2016), including factors such as methods of decision making and relationships among workplace colleagues (Koufogiannakis, 2013), which determine organizational dynamics. Other cultural enablers include respect for information as evidence, respect for information as knowledge, willingness to share information, trust in information and trust in organizational systems (Oliver, 2011). In response, Informed Systems leadership activities purposefully cultivate systemic communication and professional practices that foster and support collegial inquiry. Then co-workers can purposefully co-create information experiences and organizational knowledge that enlivens collective capacity to inform decisions, produce improvement, and sustain relationships to 'interact with, evaluate, and share information effectively and flexibly' (ACRL, 2015), 'constantly evolving organizational understanding and practice' (Hallam, Hiskens and Ong, 2014, 85).

Organizational transformation reflections

Using information to learn . . . is about being aware of the kinds of information we are using, how we are using information and how different forms of information come together to inform and transform our work.

Bruce, Hughes and Somerville, 2012, 8–9

Through this appreciative lens, Informed Systems models guide how and why organizations build human-centred communication systems for knowledge creation. Along the way, attention moves from transaction-based activities to organizational transformation outcomes enacted through intuiting, interpreting, integrating and institutionalizing knowledge (Crossan, Lane and White, 1999). As co-workers reinvent roles, responsibilities, processes and relationships, they harness the potential of reflective inquiry amidst collaborative action (Somerville, 2015a). Throughout, attention must ensure inclusive dynamics. Taking action to improve then produces changes in the ways of perceiving and of becoming newly aware and thereby learning.

Viewed through an information experience lens, colleagues collectively expand the information horizons of their work environments through wider and wider circles of consultation, co-operation and collaboration. While engaging with new information types and communication processes, they establish productive information-sharing relationships that extend beyond team boundaries through critical and creative information use and through generation and sharing of new knowledge necessary to taking purposeful action (Somerville and Mirijamdotter, 2014). Informed Systems thereby offers models for (re)learning processes, conducted within enabling systems infrastructure for collaborative information practice.

A twofold focus on Informed Learning and systems thinking, Informed Systems promotes changes in organizational awareness and behaviour through building information that leads to changes and also building ways that people use information that leads to the collective knowledge that produces changes. Building knowledge production capability in turn requires organizational design that recognizes the importance of cultivating both formal and informal interactions among individuals and with information. When individuals and groups in boundary-crossing settings exchange information and create knowledge in ever-expanding professional contexts, decision-making priorities and requisite authoritative evidence become clear. And, as colleagues learn to initiate and sustain inquiries and actions which are information-centred, action-oriented and learning-enabled, they reinvent roles, responsibilities, processes and relationships as active collaborators in the processes that enable relevant evidence to be used to make effective and efficient decisions, which co-design their future.

CHAPTER 5

Virtuality at work: an enabler of professional Information Literacy

Elham Sayyad Abdi

This chapter will discuss:

- how 'Virtuality' is that dimension of professional activity that transcends the workplace, through engagement with internet-wide communities of professional communication and practice.
- how in professions in which Virtuality is an essential component, Information Literacy (IL) can be experienced beyond workplace boundaries and in more complex ways.

Introduction

Information Literacy has been investigated in a number of professional groups in the workplace. Lawyers (Macoustra, 2004), administrative staff and academics in higher education (Bruce, 1997), senior managers (Kirk, 2004), firefighters (Lloyd, 2005), business professionals (Freudenberg, 2008), ambulance officers (Lloyd, 2009), tele-health officers (O'Farrill, 2010), web designers and developers (Sayyad Abdi, 2014; Sayyad Abdi, Partridge and Bruce, 2016) and nurses (Forster, 2015a) are examples of groups that have been investigated in terms of their experience of the phenomenon of IL in their varying working circumstances and conditions.

It has been argued that due to variations in environment and conditions, the experience of IL might be significantly different in each workplace (Lloyd and Williamson, 2008; Weiner, 2011). But is IL in fact contained and defined by the workplace? A recent study into IL experiences of web designers and developers ('web professionals' hereafter) suggested that we may be able to distinguish experienced IL in the workplace at two levels: as a workplace community and at a virtually connected, wider, professional level (Sayyad

Abdi and Bruce, 2015). IL at a professional level does not reflect necessarily the boundaries and essence of physical workspaces. People at professional level have expanded interactions which include their whole professional community of practice. This broader field of performance gives them the opportunity to encounter and recognize a wider range of information experiences than are available in and fixed by specific workplace organizational cultures. This wider information environment, using a relational approach (Bruce, 1997), can be interpreted as a more complex experience of IL. From a relational perspective, IL is about being able to use information effectively in a range of different ways in differing contexts. The ability to experience information in more varied ways, especially at those higher levels of functionality in the professional sphere, is to have a more complex experience of IL. Experiencing IL at a professional level may contribute to its enhancement. It is important, therefore, to identify and appreciate the elements of a work role that enable employees to become involved in their work at a more virtual, professional, level.

Sayyad Abdi and Bruce (2015) introduced the concept of 'Virtuality' within the work context as an element that allows individuals in a physical workplace to become involved with their community at a professional level beyond it, and therefore, experience IL in more complex ways. The present chapter, in more detail, unpacks the potential within Virtuality for giving the experience of Information Literacy a professional dimension.

This chapter should be of interest to those for whom Virtuality is a key component of their professional life. Educators and information professionals who assist such professionals might also benefit from the insights provided. Additionally, the chapter draws attention to how associated professional bodies/organizations might support the IL of their members.

Background

Workplace IL received major attention for the first time between 1995 and 1999, during an 'exploratory' phase of research by Bruce (2000). Before this, Eaton and Bawden (1991) had pointed out the importance of workplace IL by identifying information as an organizational resource and asset. Bruce specified IL as a 'significant part of the character of learning organizations as well as a key characteristic of the organization's employees' (Bruce, 1999, 33). Bruce also emphasized the importance in the workplace of the ability to deal with large quantities of information of different quality and forms, for decision making, problem solving and researching (Bruce, 2008). She pointed out the equal importance of IL when compared with information technology and computer literacy, the latter in Goad's (2002) words, 'Information Literacy's shadow'. During the past few years, the impact of IL on successful workplace performance has been acknowledged by the corporate world (Travis, 2011). The National Forum on Information Literacy (n.d.) introduced the concept of workplace IL as a key driver in achieving success at work. As a result, along with the increasing importance of IL research, a consensus on the necessity of considering IL's role in the workplace has grown (Goad, 2002; Lloyd, 2005; Perrault, 2007; Weiner, 2011).

As mentioned elsewhere in this book, the major reason why workplace IL began to attract research interest was the apparent lack of transferability of concepts from one context (i.e. education) to the other (i.e. workplace or everyday life) (Cheuk, 2008; Lloyd, 2005; Williams, Cooper and Wavell, 2014). Mutch (2008) and Leavitt (2011) and many others relate this to the different nature of the experiences in an educational setting as opposed to a workplace setting. This is of key importance, as early approaches to IL disregarded the importance of context. The complex, context-specific and open-ended information-focused tasks, characteristic of the workplace, invite researchers to describe, define and contextualize them afresh (Weiner, 2011).

Two important early efforts to reconceptualize IL in this new environment were those of Bruce (1997) and Lloyd (2005). Bruce (1997) adopted a relational view towards IL and identified seven different ways of experiencing IL in the workplace. However, her findings are mostly a reconceptualization of IL in general, rather than developing a conceptualized framework of a specific context. Instead, Lloyd's studies (2005, 2007) examined IL in the workplace through a socio-cultural approach and reconceptualized it with regard to this context. She defined IL as 'a complex socio-cultural and corporeal process that is constituted through a range of information modalities' (Lloyd, 2007). In the present chapter, IL at work is viewed from two different modalities: workplace and professional. The next section briefly describes how the two are differentiated.

Profession and workplace: two discrete contexts

A profession is described as

> a disciplined group of individuals who adhere to ethical standards and position themselves as possessing special knowledge and skills in a widely recognised body of learning derived from research, education and training at a high level, and is recognised by the public as such. A profession is also prepared to apply this knowledge and exercise these skills in the interest of others.
>
> Professions Australia, n.d.

General dictionaries define 'profession' as 'a type of job that requires special education, training, or skill' and also 'the people who work in a particular profession' (Merriam-Webster, n.d.) or 'people who do a particular type of work, considered as a group' (Cambridge English Dictionary, 2016). From these definitions, specializations as well as theoretical and practical knowledge are noted as important components that bring people in a profession together. Also it is noted that there are no boundaries except knowledge and skills that separate people from each other in a profession.

In contrast, a workplace can be defined as a *location* in which people work; e.g. an office, or a factory. A workplace can be either physical or networked. With the emergence of information and communication technologies, networked workplaces developed as supplements to physical workplaces. Teams started to work together using technology-mediated interaction. What made such networked, increasingly virtual workplaces different from physical workplaces was their ability to assist teams to overcome geographical and temporal boundaries. The team component, however, is still the same. Whether it is in a physical or virtual workplace, people, as a team, aim to complete a set of assigned tasks defined by their employer as their day-to-day work.

Comparing the two notions of profession and workplace, one of the important elements that distinguishes the two is how people relate to, and interact with, each other. While there are no boundaries to restrict teams in a professional space, there are within a workplace environment. In a particular profession, it is specific knowledge, skills, competence or expertise in a specific field that are the basis of their common identity; whereas in a workplace, it is a set of activities designed to be accomplished within a particular enterprise. Professionals are considered as a broad community of practice, while workplaces have 'employees'.

Two different contexts for experiencing Information Literacy

The study of web professionals' IL experiences (Sayyad Abdi, 2014) mentioned above, suggested that IL for this group was experienced in a wider 'professional' context in addition to a localized workplace one. In fact, participants rarely talked about their immediate workspaces and day-to-day interactions with their colleagues. Rather, they reflected more upon their extensive interactions with many and varied information sources and numerous categories and constituencies of the people that populated the web professional community of practice. Information Literacy seemed to be experienced quite differently in these two contexts (Sayyad Abdi and Bruce, 2015).

A workspace has its own components. It includes physical components (such as a building) which are sometimes technologically connected to form a digital workplace, and also policies and procedures to follow. Information flows within, in and out of the identified work environment. These components constitute the context in which individuals will experience IL at a workplace level. A 'profession-oriented' workspace has additional key components, such as translocational peer groups, a shared professional literature and a sense of profession-wide achievement, purpose and value. These different components result in professions providing a slightly different context for IL experiences compared to the workplace itself. While people work in teams in the workplace, they do not have to necessarily belong to a team at a professional level. It is mainly shared knowledge and expertise that bring people together in a profession.

One of the factors that distinguish a profession and its associated work environments is the variety and richness of IL experiences it facilitates and promotes. A profession is constituted from a range of individuals coming from different workplaces but with shared areas of interest and operation. They bring their knowledge, expertise, skills and varying workplace-specific cultures of information engagement to share with, and develop through, the community. This variation of practice and intensity of knowledge helps members of the community develop awareness of a wider and richer information environment and work dimensionality. Due to the potential involvement of the whole profession within a specific field, an intensity of collaboration, learning and widening of perspective is likely to occur. The result is a complex and effective sourcing of information and a unique and fitted-for-purpose information culture. These contacts within a broader information environment result in deeper and more varied engagement with information and information use. At a professional level, individuals have more people to interact with, more varied situations to be involved in and therefore more opportunities to engage with information. Each member of the community of practice introduces and shares their understanding of IL. Professionals have ongoing encounters with many different ways of using information and have the chance to observe how other members of the community of practice engage with information.

According to the relational perspective (Bruce, 1997) that views IL as using information effectively in a range of different ways, it can be argued here that *engaging with information at a professional level enhances variation in IL experience.* A person with the ability to experience IL in a wide range of contexts is more likely to adopt *the* most effective way to engage with information in a specific situation.

So far we have discussed the distinction between experiencing IL in two different work contexts: the workplace context and the professional context. We have emphasized the likelihood of the richness of the experiences at the professional level. We will now analyse that richness in more detail. The analysis will be of interest to workplace and professional IL education stakeholders, allowing them to identify tools to help support Information Literacy in their professional clients.

Virtual workplace v. Virtuality at work

Virtuality has up to now been mainly addressed in the literature as a team phenomenon, one of the characteristics of team dynamics in contrast to face-to-face interaction. Concepts such as virtual team and Virtuality have been subjects of investigation. According to Shu, Tu and Wang (2011) the most frequent contributing factors to virtual collaboration identified by the research have been:

1 geographic distribution of team members, (i.e. being in different sites, offices, countries)
2 temporal distribution of team members (e.g. being in different time-zones that do not permit overlapping work hours)
3 technological infrastructure that supports co-operative communication and interaction.

Dixon and Panteli (2010), in a discussion of technology-mediated interaction in contrast to traditional face-to-face interaction, adopted the term 'virtuality in teams' to replace 'virtual team'. This expression is thought to better define the increasingly hybrid nature of interaction in teams, where face-to-face interaction and technology-mediated interaction are often experienced in conjunction. Such virtual continuities are seen as a solution to those boundaries for communication and interaction which result from differences in physical location, time-zone, language, culture, knowledge and work practice. Dixon and Panteli also noted the value that Virtuality adds in workplaces. They suggested that recognizing Virtuality at work increases acknowledgement of the knowledge and skills obtained by individuals at work, through recognition of those teams existing beyond their employer's organization.

The concept 'Virtuality' put forward in this chapter is not that of virtual workspaces. A virtual workspace is a virtual space in which people in the same organization or partner organizations connect to and collaborate with each other on a regular basis. In comparison, Virtuality is about the work context rather than the workspace. It is more about the context in which professionals practice rather the location they work in. In that sense, Virtuality is an inherent element of work practice in a specific profession and is recognized as part of the nature of that profession's practice. More specifically, it is considered as essential to, integrated in and unified and intertwined around the practice of individuals in that specific profession. Virtuality, therefore, does not refer to virtual teams versus face-to-face teams, but is a component of practice in a profession that is integral and essential.

The World Organisation of Webmasters (WebProfessionals.org) defines webmasters as those who create, manage and market websites. These include web designers, web developers, web marketers and analysts of all kinds of websites. The environment in which they work is the world wide web, one of the broadest virtual environments. It can be said that the virtual environment of the world wide web creates both a context and the key medium for the practice of this group of professionals who may not be employed by the same organization but who collaborate by exchanging ideas, methods of practice and information sources.

How does such a work environment, in which Virtuality is central, facilitate IL experience at a professional level?

Virtuality: an enabler of professional Information Literacy

Findings from the research study into their IL experiences (Sayyad Abdi, 2014) showed that as creators of the web itself, the nature of web professionals' work has a strongly embedded Virtuality component. A web professional works on and for the broad web environment. The web is the main work platform, one which brings together a strong virtually connected community of practice. Web professionals are members of very active online forums and possess active social media accounts, in fact communicate with fellow practitioners in the field through many different online channels. In such a community, individuals were shown to be in close contact with each other across the whole web industry. The fact that the community of practice of the web industry is an online space enabled the study's participants in different parts of the industry to interact with each other at a professional level with more ease and convenience.

Web professionals' experience of IL can be categorized in four different ways:

- Category 1: staying informed
- Category 2: building a successful website
- Category 3: solving a problem
- Category 4: participating in a community of practice.

When describing their experiences of IL, web professionals in two of the four categories (i.e. Categories 1 and 4), strongly referred to the profession, rather than the workplace, as the context in which they experience their IL. In Category 1, when talking about staying informed as one way of experiencing IL, research participants mentioned the wide information environment surrounding them as the space they scan to keep current.

The widest part of the ring in Figure 5.1 on the next page represents this space. The wider information environment is the space in which most relevant information flows and web workers stay most firmly connected to, i.e. the

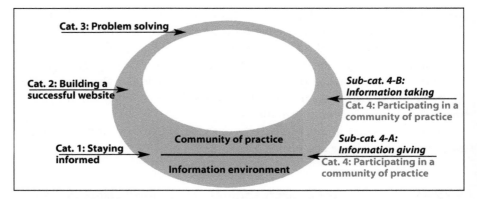

Figure 5.1 *Information literacy as experienced by web professionals*

whole profession. It is the same professional-level space from which web professionals capture useful information to build a knowledge base for future use.

Also, in Category 4, research participants maintained a strong focus on the broad community of practice discussed above. Web professionals actively talked about the broad community of practice as the most relevant and common source of information. In two sub-categories of Category 4, information giving (Sub-category 4-A) and information taking (Sub-category 4-B), web professionals talked about people they learnt from and informed. The research participants rarely turned their attention to people at work, i.e. people in teams they were working with on a daily basis, when talking about information sharing.

The results from the study suggested that it was actually the Virtuality of the web work that facilitated the relevant and necessary range of experience of IL that allowed any degree of professional functionality to occur. Having the web as a work environment, research participants described the use of online forums, social networks and online channels, places they would go for their day-to-day problem solving, and as the means through which leaders in the field communicated with and 'taught' field practitioners. Hence Virtuality can be seen as a necessary enabler of IL at that level of complexity and ambition required by professionals who are reaching out into new ways of using information to develop a creative and wide-reaching horizon of practice. That is, by taking advantage of Virtuality a richer experience of IL can be provided.

Discussion and conclusion

The importance of IL in the workplace has been suggested by those researchers who have concentrated on how it informs best practice. Sayyad Abdi and Bruce (2015) have highlighted a 21st-century aspect to the modern workplace by suggesting a distinction between the experience of IL in a localized 'workplace' (even if networked) and the translocal, digitally focused, professional context. This chapter has highlighted the distinction between the workplace and the professional information environment through highlighting the comparative broadness of the professional constituency. Workplace IL is based on information-related practices occurring at physical or virtually connected workplaces, while professional IL is concerned with effective information experiences amongst the broader community of practice. Such comparisons draw our attention to the importance and value of experiencing IL at that professional level which facilitates the depth and richness of experience of which it is capable.

Virtuality can provide more solid engagement between members of a community of practice and stronger involvement in a broader information environment compared to the workplace. There are a range of professions that have Virtuality as an essential and regular component through which members engage with and transform their everyday professional practice. It can be asserted that this is the definition of a modern profession.

It is recommended that other work contexts are identified and studied through an IL lens in order to build upon the findings of the study discussed here. Such research would not only advance our understanding of how the different workplace and professional IL contexts are experienced, but also shed further light into the theoretical understanding of the role Virtuality plays in enabling IL at a professional level.

Moreover, further research is suggested to examine to what extent Virtuality could be imported into work contexts that do not necessarily have this component. It should be considered how application of tools such as social media in work contexts without an existing virtual component could enhance communication. It should be noted whether social media or similar virtual tools could bring employees the engagement they require to become involved with their peers and with relevant information sources in that broader information environment surrounding the community of practice. When embedded into work contexts the impact of Virtuality on IL experience should be studied.

Professional bodies should consider taking advantage of Virtuality to support and nurture the IL of their members. As organizations that look after the whole communities of practice of particular professions, professional bodies can introduce and embed Virtuality, if not directly and as a requirement of the work context, at least as a recommended component of professional practice. Through such implementation, professional communities of practice will transcend the workplace and communicate and challenge each other. In such communities, all members of a profession find the opportunity to engage with each other and share their knowledge and their most recent best practice with the rest of the community. Such a supportive virtual information environment has the potential to bring people of a field together and expose them to new and multiple ways of experiencing information and engaging with information, far more than they experience in their workplaces. This results in a professional becoming aware of more effective ways of using information that have been adopted by other members of the community and consequently more complex ways of experiencing IL.

This process of awareness can be considered as an educational process that might be of interest to educators and advocates of IL who can take advantage of Virtuality as a tool in work-related IL education. Educators can apply Variation Theory (Marton and Booth, 1997) (also see Chapter 11) and learning studies (Lo, 2012; Pang and Marton, 2003) which defines learning as a shift in view that allows an individual to see things in a different way to design opportunities through Virtuality, so that individuals understand and apply the recognized ways of experiencing IL in their community of practice.

Virtuality is one of the elements identified as an enabler of IL at a professional level. What are the other work-world elements that might give additional dimensions to 'professional' IL? Further research is necessary.

CHAPTER 6

Determining the value of Information Literacy for employers

Stéphane Goldstein and Andrew Whitworth

This chapter will discuss:

- how the value of Information Literacy in the workplace might be increased by employing and training individuals who have appropriate and relevant know-how, competency and awareness in the handling of information, in whatever form that takes.
- how that value might also be increased by deploying processes and creating environments that help to foster effective uses of data and information.

Introduction

This chapter discusses the value of Information Literacy (IL) in the workplace. It draws from the conclusions of a study that considered, in the setting of a small range of enterprises, the value that is added by employing and training individuals who have appropriate and relevant know-how, competency and awareness in the handling of information, in whatever form that takes; and in deploying processes and creating environments that help to foster effective uses of data and information. The value might be financial, but it might also relate to other factors that are important to enterprises, such as enhanced efficiency, competitive advantage or employee job satisfaction. These questions bear a close relation to the long-standing debate about the impact of IL instruction in school and higher education settings (Todd, 1995; Streatfield and Markless, 2008); we can similarly ask whether and how information know-how contributes to the well-being of enterprises.

The chapter introduces a practical approach to addressing these questions, and should therefore be relevant to enterprises across all sectors (commercial, public and not-for-profit), and particularly to those within enterprises with responsibility for human resources, training and skills, information/data management and financial management. It is also relevant for information professionals (particularly those in the workplace), information scientists and all those with an interest in the contribution of information, data and knowledge to the workings of enterprises.

Background

Recent literature reviews by Williams, Cooper and Wavell (2014) and Inskip (2014) have discussed the importance of IL in the workplace. The reviews counter the bias in the IL literature towards perceiving it narrowly as information-searching competencies of the kind that are deployed in higher education settings (Whitworth, 2014, 74–81). IL can be generally defined as the capacity to make *critical judgements* about information, and this capacity can be learned. Workplace learning, however, is less structured and more collaborative than most formalized educational settings. The IL skills and know-how that are valued in workplaces are context-specific, rooted not in standards and generic guidance, but in practice and the 'intersubjective agreement' of different stakeholders in the setting (Lloyd, 2010; 2012). There is a greater emphasis on people (as opposed to texts) as information sources; thus, developing an understanding of workplace IL practice means appreciating: the social and informal ways in which information is processed into knowledge; good information management and organization; and data security (Williams, Cooper and Wavell, 2014, 2–3). As Inskip says (2014, 9): 'This complexity requires a paradigm shift away from IL as a list of skills to be acquired and towards an understanding of the information environment in which the practice sits.'

Seeking IL in the workplace is also complicated by difficulties with the term 'Information Literacy' itself. Conley and Gill (2011) and Inskip (2014, 6) reported that business professionals recognized IL elements, but only when identified separately from the umbrella term. For example, Heichman Taylor (2008) reports that 'critical thinking' was identified by employers as a key constituent of staff members' capacity to make critical judgements and thus maintain, or steward, local 'information landscapes' (Lloyd, 2010; Wenger, White and Smith, 2009). 'Environmental scanning' (Zhang, Majid and Foo, 2010) was identified as a business process facilitated by these judgements. But these elements are themselves often vaguely defined, and their costs and benefits hard to isolate and measure, directly or indirectly.

Nevertheless, evidence exists to confirm the value of IL, and associated factors, in a range of workplace settings. Cheuk (2002) seeks to demonstrate how promotion of company-wide knowledge creation, sharing and use – and the critical IL competencies that underpin these – can lead to greater operational efficiency and the exploitation of business opportunities. Organizational competitiveness and profitability may also be enhanced through developing competence within the enterprise to use information effectively (Cheuk, 1998), and a strategic approach to meeting organizational information needs (Sen and Taylor, 2007). The fostering among staff of confidence and competence in interacting with information is also shown to add critical business value (Cheuk, 2008). For some professions, such as law, the impact and significance of accurate and timely information are a key contributor to companies' success in the marketplace, and the information know-how of lawyers underpins this (Gasteen and O'Sullivan, 2000). Conversely, in information-rich workplaces, inadequate functional IL among employees results in a noticeably less efficient workforce (Hepworth and Walton, 2013). And a number of further studies show how IL helps to address significant organizational challenges, such as dealing with information overload (O'Sullivan, 2002), formulating adaptive strategies for coping with uncertainties (Zhang, Majid and Foo, 2010), better informed decision making (Grieves, 1998) and ensuring Evidence-based Practice in particular sectors such as healthcare (Ayre, 2006).

A full picture of an organization's IL environment should also account for how the architecture of information systems, and of the physical space of offices, meeting rooms and so on, affect information flows (cf. Tagliaventi and Mattarelli, 2006). One's position in social networks has long been recognized as influencing how easily or not one can access information (e.g. Granovetter, 1973), and this is particularly true in workplace environments, where tacit knowledge plays a more significant role in making informational judgements than it does in formal educational settings. As Lloyd (2010; 2012) and Wenger (1998; Wenger, White and Smith, 2009) recognize, the informational practices and critical judgements that constantly shape the 'information landscape' or 'digital habitat' (that is, information and digital literacy) are also collective, and thus intersubjective; paradigms of IL which concentrate on individual facility with information fail to recognize IL's communitarian aspects (Harris, 2008).

Thus, determining the value of IL for employers requires more than just an audit of the costs and benefits of (individualized) training in IL skills, as these are typically conceived in the literature. In 2007, de Saulles (2007) estimated that poor IL cost UK businesses alone £3.7bn per year, but though this figure provides a useful indicator of the overall, and potential, return on investment (ROI) in developing IL in workplaces, more detail is required to answer questions such as: what benefits do employers derive from recruiting, retaining and developing individuals and communities of practice who are information-literate? What return on investment would organizations derive by providing relevant training to their employees, and better recognizing IL, or aspects of it, in the professional and career development of their employees? What does the IL of employees – at all levels – add to the performance of enterprises in the private, public and not-for-profit sectors? As recognized by Williams, Cooper and Wavell (2014), greater evidence of impact of IL, expressed in terms that relate to industry and professional priority areas is urgently needed if business, government and professions are to be convinced of the relevance and significance of IL.

Approach

To help address these questions, there is a need for practical approaches that can help enterprises themselves to reflect on the place of IL in their strategies, policies, cultures and practices; and crucially, to help them understand and appreciate its relevance to their organizational priorities. The DeVIL project (Determining the Value of Information Literacy) provides one such approach. DeVIL has produced a practical output: a tangible resource, in the form of a prototype tool whose variables allow for the identification of value as set against six main areas of investment by organizations. It sets out a method that provides, through the prism of a small sample of enterprises, a means of identifying areas of workplace activity where investment in IL adds value; and it provides an opportunity for initiating some reflection on how and where IL contributes to the well-being of enterprises. The tool is available online at www.informall.org.uk/employment/il-value/il-value-tool.

The DeVIL project is relatively small-scale and should be seen as only the first stage in a more extensive programme of research into how the value of IL can be determined in specific workplace settings. It took place between March and July 2015 and was funded by the UK's Chartered Institute of Information and Library Professionals (CILIP) Information Literacy Group (ILG). Its aim was to perform an initial scan of selected workplace IL environments, to determine:

- how employers perceive the value of information know-how, competencies and skills in specific contexts
- what formal and informal training and staff development programmes take place within the workplace that are, directly or indirectly, oriented towards information
- what organizational practices (both inward and outward facing) are in place to promote the effective and smart use, handling and sharing of information, and to foster a culture that encourages this
- where possible, what relevant data might be collected by organizations, as part of their everyday operations, that could subsequently be used to

calculate or estimate returns on investments into developing information know-how, competencies and skills.

The project was founded on three case studies, intended to reflect the variety of employment sectors:

- Case study A was a large, public sector organization: an inner-city local authority with around 4000 staff. It is responsible for a diverse portfolio of activities, including housing, social care and management of the local environment, and a very broad spectrum of information flows into, around and back out of the organization.
- Case study B was a small, private sector company that develops and markets a human resources information system for use in the corporate sector. It has grown in the last ten years from a 'one-man band' to now employing around 30 staff, many of them part-time.
- Case study C represented the voluntary sector, being a small organization that acts as an information broker, training centre and supplier of software solutions to voluntary sector organizations throughout a large metropolitan area. It also has around 30 staff.

The project generated data that permit a broad understanding of workplace information environments, and the way IL is constructed and valued in these environments. In the first instance, reports, policy documents and statements from the three cases were examined. This initial analysis formed the basis of interviews in each of the three cases with key management personnel, representing a range of relevant areas within their respective organizations: information policy and governance; information systems; human resources; staff development; and finance.

Findings

The analysis of the data allowed for the identification of five broad sets of business value factors that can be said to be influenced by IL. These are:

1 returns measured in terms of increased efficiency
2 improved profitability
3 better customer/client service
4 improvements to the motivation and morale of staff
5 maximized compliance with relevant legal and/or regulatory regimes.

Each of these areas may be broken down into more specific factors, relating to the value propositions flagged up in the three cases. This is summarized in Figure 6.1, which presents a schematic picture of aspects of operations where information-literate practices are likely to add value and deliver returns.

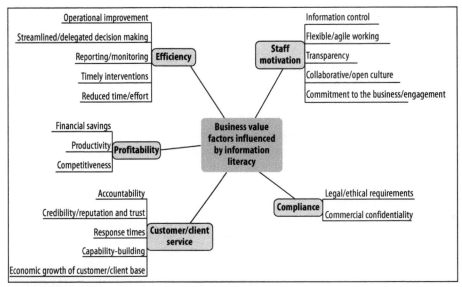

Figure 6.1 *Value propositions relevant to Information Literacy*

The value factors make up one side of the prototype tool referred to above. A second set of factors may be drawn from the analysis of the cases, identifying the particular components of business investment to which the value factors relate. The DeVIL project has thus identified five categories of investment:

1   investments in staff development, support and guidance, organizational culture
2   investments in information systems, technologies and representations
3   investments in practices
4   investments in use of space
5   investments in outreach and client relations.

Each is discussed in more detail below.

Investment in staff development, support and guidance and organizational culture

All three case study organizations invest in staff development and in the fostering of organizational cultures, with a direct impact on the way that staff members relate to business data and information. This commitment is set out explicitly in relevant strategic documents: case A's Digital Strategy allows for 'education, awareness, etc. for staff about the integrity, validity and intent of internet information'; C's Strategic Plan talks about fostering 'an internal culture of experimentation and curiosity'. However, the approaches vary between the organizations.

As might be expected in a large and complex organization that has to comply with a broad range of statutory requirements, formal training in IL-related issues takes place in A to address areas that are mandatory for local authorities, such as training on protocols and processes needed to ensure data security and confidentiality, covering sensitive areas such as child protection; this is what A terms 'transactional' training. The training may be face-to-face where it is important for staff to demonstrate appropriate knowledge, but is also done online. Organization A has developed interactive tests (that are in the process of being made mandatory) on information management and data security. Transactional learning is also used to develop expertise in specific tools such as Yammer (A's enterprise social network). In some specific cases, high-level information competences are achieved through professional qualifications, notably CISSP (Certified Information Systems Security Professional). There is also an expectation that staff will become familiar with statutory and ethical requirements regarding the handling of data, as outlined in A's extensive guidance. A network of different categories of experts, located in different departments, is available to provide advice where this is needed; these are known as Information Asset Owners, Local Information Managers and Data Stewards. It follows that different aspects of data literacy are crucial to enable staff to meet many of A's obligations to its clients as a public service provider.

C also engages with this sort of training, but geared less to its staff than to the client base (voluntary organizations within the city region). C exists to make the local voluntary sector more informed, and enable it to use information effectively; it aims to 'foster an internal culture of experimentation and curiosity' among its clients. As such, outreach activities, including training courses and briefings (for instance, in data protection), form part of C's efforts to empower its clients, impart reliable information to them and thereby equip them with appropriate business know-how. C also requires its staff members to '[build] intelligence and understanding of and for the voluntary sector – carrying out research, collecting and disseminating information and ideas'.

B is too small a company to run formal training; for an SME of its size, it is not cost-effective to run or to send its staff on face-to-face and/or residential courses. Instead, the focus is allowing its staff up to 40 hours per year to make use of modular, online courses. However, it runs semi-structured, internal masterclasses where staff members are encouraged to share know-how in groups, and where such know-how is demonstrated and explained. It also runs an apprenticeship scheme, with one individual currently in post. But even for B, it is imperative to ensure that its staff members have the know-how to care for certain types of sensitive information: the company recognizes the importance of knowledge of protocols and processes needed to protect the confidentiality of customers' data.

Less formal approaches to acquisition of skills and knowledge – and to the fostering of a culture characterized by extensive information sharing – are characteristic of both A and B. They therefore present similarities in spite of the differences in business purpose and scale. Case A deploys what it terms a 70/20/10 approach to training. Of the overall training activity, 10% aims to be 'transactional' (see above), and 20% takes the form of online courses. The remaining 70% relies on learning through colleagues, by osmosis and/or learning by doing. There is an explicit commitment to take people out of their 'comfort zone' and put them into places where skills are developed and immediately applied, for example, leadership events, directorate management teams, presenting at board level. This is learning that is cost-neutral to the organization but stretches the staff, makes them feel motivated and engaged. This 70/20/10 spectrum thereby blurs the distinction between formal training and the informal acquisition of know-how, over time, through more casual forms of interfacing. Tools such as Yammer encourage the regular, informal exchange of knowledge, breaking down the formal, hierarchical chains of command and information flow. Communities of practice develop, founded on a culture of openness and transparency, and a readiness to share information. Staff are stimulated into using (and learning how to use) delegated means of sharing information, without the need for formal training, because it works for them – and also because they want to keep up with their peers and managers.

For B, given the relative absence of structured training, there is a reliance on staff learning and expanding their knowledge base in less formal ways. The open, collaborative nature of the organization, along with a strong inbuilt sense of teamwork, facilitates the effective flow of information within the company, and between it and its customers. Having relevant information at hand is important for ensuring good levels of customer service, and staff are expected to be all-rounders to deal with the full range of customer interactions – with regard to both technical knowledge and soft skills, such as the ability to communicate with customers in a language which the latter can relate to. It is therefore important for staff to keep themselves constantly informed about evolving customer systems, products, needs and expectations; about the rapidly changing technological environment (particularly important for front-end developers); and also about what their competitors are up to.

Cases A and B rely also on the deployment of in-house experts, or champions, to advise and guide their staff. Case A has sufficient critical mass to make provision for specialist services that support its digital strategy; these function through four centres of excellence relating to agile working, business intelligence/open data, customer experience and data join up/collaborating with partners. Similarly, expert support is also at hand to help with areas such as information governance. The same critical mass also allows A the resources to formulate detailed guidance on information management, information security, data protection and the use of social networking. This sort of well developed corporate documentation is less likely to be a factor for smaller organizations, and neither B nor C offer such material to their staff. B makes use of staff expertise to provide informal in-house training, focused on technical skills. B also runs semi-structured masterclasses where staff members are encouraged to share know-how in groups, and where such know-how is demonstrated and explained – an instance of the use of peer networks to develop staff know-how.

Investments in information systems, technologies and representations

Case A has by far the biggest investment in information systems. The multiplicity and complexity of these systems has led the local authority to push for systemic improvements in three broad areas, all involving the concomitant acquisition by staff of information-related skills:

1 Making data more readily available and shareable through systems designed to allow staff to control and manipulate it in a delegated fashion: this allows them to make use of, interpret and analyse data relating to service delivery, rather than pass it on through the line management chain, as would have been the case in the past. There is thus improved management of data by a large number of staff members, and more intelligent and critical use of it to gauge performance and impact.

2 Integrating data so that staff may deploy it in a more seamless and holistic way for the benefit of clients: this means that data about the local authority's clients and/or users that were once scattered are now increasingly brought together to provide a rounded view of the needs of each case.

3 Deploying business collaboration and networking tools. Yammer was introduced in order to change the way that information is exchanged across the organization. It is an example of a system being implemented strategically with the very clear aim of effecting the changes in organizational culture outlined above.

For C, investment in information systems is on a much smaller scale. It trains its clients in the use of CiviCRM, contact management software designed to meet their diverse data management needs. Over 50 clients are presently being supported with this software. C offers consultancy to identify each client's data needs and how they manage relevant information. Clients vary greatly, so C sets up and configures the software according to those needs, and after set-up, provides training to clients' staff. This is a paid service, acting as a social enterprise which can support other work undertaken by C.

Case B's core business is developing an information system for use by other organizations, but beyond applications such as financial accounting software, there is no particular use made of information systems to govern the company's work processes.

Investments in practices

Cases A and B in particular deploy a range of practices intended to facilitate the handling of information and data and the ability to make critical judgements about relevance and significance. All such practices require a degree of know-how on the part of staff who are expected to ensure that information flows efficiently, that it reaches or is passed through the correct channels, and that ethics, laws, confidentiality and other statutory requirements are not breached. Therefore, there is a mutual connection between this and the first category of investment, into staff and the organizational culture. However, what this category captures are those investments which are made in new or revised procedures, protocols and standards for information handling within the organization.

There is a particularly strong emphasis, in different settings, on the importance of information and data sharing between individuals or departments within the organization, for instance for improved business intelligence, or to support the provision of joined-up services. The latter factor is associated with the aggregation of data from different business sources in order to present a more holistic view of client needs, and to break down barriers that retard the movement of information between different internal databanks, sources and operational units. Investment in developing and supporting these practices allows for the provision of a more seamless and professional service to clients, thereby making it easier to intervene preventively through deriving a fuller and more rounded picture of client needs. Joining up of data may also have a further beneficial effect, with a very direct financial value for organization A: it can lead to the reduction of fraud by identifying cases where undesirable practices (e.g. subletting of property) are only revealed through juxtaposing different data and information sources. To achieve effective sharing and aggregation, it is obviously important for staff to ensure that inputted data is of good quality, reducing the scope for mistakes and avoiding the need for expensive and time-consuming data cleansing.

Many practices revolve around the need to ensure information security and the protection of sensitive or commercially confidential data, safeguarding information for instance through security protocols. There may be an obligation to ensure that information is given out rapidly and efficiently: systems and practices therefore need to be in place to ensure responsiveness, with a capacity to respond readily and quickly to client enquiries and requests for information (including, in the case of public bodies such as A, freedom of information requests). Case A also deploys a 'right first time' approach to answering such requests.

Investments in use of space

In two case studies it was plain that information management and, thus, IL was facilitated by the spatial configuration of their premises. Both A and B have open-plan offices, and both rely on the nature of the spatial environment to help foster a particular type of working culture that is founded on an aptitude to share information, particularly across departmental or team boundaries. In case A, the local authority has recently moved into a large new building, designed to a high specification to encourage new, less hierarchical ways of working and to provide cost savings on accommodation. The building is smaller than its predecessor, as the authority promotes flexible, home and/or off-site working using mobile devices, and so the building is not large enough to contain its full complement of staff at any one time. 'Hot-desking' is the norm, and the use of paper has been reduced to a bare minimum. Careful design and use of space helps to create an informal and flexible working environment, designed to capitalize on conversations between small groups of staff members with no fixed work-stations; it encourages agile working and the breaking down of silos. In this way, the physical working environment contributes to culture shift and to the way that information is shared and exchanged.

In the case of B, the office is considerably smaller, and has not been specifically designed for the company, but the ethos remains the same: an open space which deliberately serves as a venue for facilitating links between teams and the sharing of information. Small areas reserved for leisure activities reinforce the informal nature of the environment. For C, however, the creative use of office space to facilitate information sharing is not an evident factor.

Investments in outreach and client relations

Information flows, in both directions, between the organization and its customers/clients must be accounted for when determining the value of IL to each. All three organizations are attentive to their client or customer base, and rely on well informed staff to ensure good relationships with these external stakeholders. For A and C, the empowerment of users is an important factor. Case A has a mandate to reduce digital exclusion, and takes steps to develop digital skills in the community, for instance through the use of local 'digital champions': residents in housing estates, supported by the local authority, who undertake outreach work to engage with their more digitally excluded neighbours. Council services, such as libraries, and volunteer networks are also used for such purposes. A's Digital Strategy states that, 'By tapping into the rich and diverse talent pool that exists in [the locality] including our volunteers, third sector and local business we can add capacity to develop digital confidence and life skills'.

For C, there is a similar capacity-building imperative, to build and expand the capacity of the voluntary sector to operate in a business-like way – particularly important in a financial context where voluntary organizations are increasingly being called upon to play a greater role in local service delivery. Indeed, the very nature of the organization leads it to capitalize on its ability to nurture its client base; the capacity to impart reliable information is crucial for this. B also gains from having an information-literate customer base, in terms of getting high-quality feedback, for instance about potential new product development. There is thus a relationship between ensuring that customers are well informed about B's products and their applicability, and future business opportunities.

Towards calculations of returns on investment in IL

Value propositions under the *profitability* and *efficiency* headings are often expressed quantitatively, in terms of direct costs, though the specific financial data are not always easy to come by, either because the organization is too small to generate them or, at the other end of the scale, because of the size and complexity of case A, and its legacy of multiple, and not always complementary, information systems. Some data were available from case A: for example, the move to the new office and the parallel project to adopt new information practices saved £10 million. Similar quantitative data may be available in other cases.

Other costs are more indirect, or potential. Giving staff greater access to and control of relevant data (and hence business intelligence) allows for improved accountability and enhanced monitoring and reporting. This not only generates more efficiency through time saving, but allows for the potential stripping of management layers through more devolved ways of working. Failure to meet regulatory standards may result in fines. The local authority A had never been found culpable in any breach of data protection standards, thus not subjected to fines from the UK Information Commissioner, but the potential remains. B and C, at smaller absolute scales but no less importantly in relative terms, acted as custodians of client data and would both lose valuable credibility and trust if poor information-handling practices on the part of their staff were to result in data loss or breaches of security or privacy. This would in turn impact on reputation, and the companies' ability to acquire repeat or new business from customers. Therefore, investments in information-literate practices are here akin to 'preventive maintenance', with the benefits measured in terms of the reduction of the risk of incurring costs at a later date due to poor information handling.

Staff turnover is an important cost to account for. There is a direct financial cost associated with replacing staff and a substantial indirect cost, as well. As previously noted, a great deal of the information that is embedded in any workplace landscape is tacit, stored in the minds and embodied in the practices of colleagues (Lloyd, 2010; 2012). Even in case A, with its substantial investment in information systems, not all the valuable information can be captured and made explicit, and staff members' accumulated knowledge of matters such as to whom information requests should be directed would be lost if that person were to leave. In the smaller organizations this problem is many times more acute. Thus, investments in staff to develop their information know-how are perceived as having returns in the shape of job satisfaction and motivation. Staff who feel valued and that they can develop their careers in the organization are more likely to stay and thus keep their tacit knowledge within the landscape.

Offering effective customer/client service, and preserving credibility and trust, also brings returns on investment in terms of the organization's interactions with its environment in ways that keep that environment sustainable, so that the organization can continue to draw resources from it. Local authority A seeks to build IL in its residents partly to optimize solutions like new information systems and thus drive internal efficiency gains, but it also undertakes this work to enhance their employability, and thus sustain the economic potential of the locality. C also seeks to increase the capacity of its client base and thus address its own sustainability. Such returns on investment must be calculated on a much longer term than is typical in direct financial accounting.

The DeVIL tool

The essential purpose of the prototype DeVIL tool is to illustrate how IL adds value to enterprises, allowing cross-referencing between areas of investment and potential returns, and providing detail on specific examples of such investment. The tool was developed as a means of presenting, in a practical format, the findings of the study. As such, it can reflect only the evidence gathered in the context of the limited number of case studies, but it has the potential to help develop the evidence base on the benefits of IL in the workplace, and thereby demonstrate to a range of stakeholders – including businesses themselves – that IL is an important contributor to the capacity of enterprises to thrive and innovate.

The tool is articulated around the five broad value propositions set out in Figure 6.2 opposite. These propositions should be instantly recognizable to any enterprise, whatever the sector. They therefore allow IL to be couched in terms that employers can relate to. Associated with the propositions, and branching from them, are the 20 indicators of value also outlined in Figure 6.1 (page 72). These are the building blocks, at the heart of the tool, which set out how value – in its various forms – may be achieved.

The tool takes the form of a spreadsheet (Figure 6.2). The columns to the left are the tabular representation of Figure 6.1, and they list the value propositions and their indicators of value. The row at the top represents the areas of investment described above. The cells below the row therefore allow for the insertion of specific factors, relevant to IL, that illustrate the correlation between given indicators of value and areas of investment. The tool also provides brief but more detailed explanation of these factors and of their relevance to IL. Filters provide an element of interactivity. By focusing on a particular factor under a given area of investment, it becomes possible to identify easily which are the relevant indicators of value. For instance, under 'practices', fraud reduction is flagged in association with two indicators of value: financial savings and legal/ethical requirements. Filters may also be applied on the indicators of value themselves, to provide a view of all the factors associated with any given indicator. A short set of illustrated explanatory notes have been produced to provide basic guidance in the use of the tool; this is also available at www.informall.org.uk/employment/il-value.

The tool therefore provides a means to navigate around a basic map of indicators of value for enterprises, and to pick out IL-related factors corresponding to particular sorts of value. It is not designed to calculate the value or return on investment of information-literate workforces in quantitative terms. As we have seen, it would require a more comprehensive and detailed study to derive such findings. Instead, the tool allows enterprises and other interested parties to chart the relationship between how organizations perceive value and factors related to the competent and professional handling of information and data.

	Main value propositions	Indicators of value	Staff development, support / guidance, organisational culture	Information systems, technologies, representations	Areas of investment — Practices	Use of space	Outreach, client relations
3	1. Efficiency	1.1 Organisational improvement		Data quality			
4	1. Efficiency	1.1 Organisational improvement		Using data-derived indicators			
5	1. Efficiency	1.1 Organisational improvement		Maintaining currency			
6	1. Efficiency	1.1 Organisational improvement					Use of feedback
7	1. Efficiency	1.1 Organisational improvement	Deployment of experts	Use of designated in-house experts or champions, e.g. through digital centres of excellence [A3] [A4] [A5] [A9] [B1]			
8	1. Efficiency	1.2 Streamlined / delegated decision making	Sought-after skills				
9	1. Efficiency	1.2 Streamlined / delegated decision making		Data analytics			
10	1. Efficiency	1.2 Streamlined / delegated decision making					
11	1. Efficiency	1.2 Streamlined / delegated decision making			Delegating to staff		
12	1. Efficiency	1.2 Streamlined / delegated decision making	Deployment of experts				
13	1. Efficiency	1.3 Reporting /monitoring	Data literacy				
14	1. Efficiency	1.3 Reporting /monitoring	Deployment of experts				
15	1. Efficiency	1.3 Reporting /monitoring		Accounting systems		Allowing more staff to handle data – potential for cutting out management layers [A1] [A2]	
16	1. Efficiency	1.3 Reporting /monitoring		Data analytics	Using data-derived indicators		
17	1. Efficiency	1.3 Reporting /monitoring		Deployment of data analysis and visualisation tools such as ClikView, allowing for better access to and easier control of data and information [A1] [A2]			
18	1. Efficiency	1.3 Reporting/monitoring	Data literacy				
19	1. Efficiency	1.3 Reporting/monitoring					Business intelligence
20	1. Efficiency	1.4 Timely interventions			Maintaining currency		
21	1. Efficiency	1.5 Reduced time/effort			Data aggregation		
22	1. Efficiency	1.5 Reduced time/effort		Data analytics			
23	1. Efficiency	1.5 Reduced time/effort			Data/information sharing		
24	1. Efficiency	1.5 Reduced time/effort			Data aggregation		

Figure 6.2 *The DeVIL tool*

The intention of the tool is to provide the basis for dialogue and investigation of diverse workplace contexts, rather than generalized figures for returns on investment. It can help identify areas in which returns may not have been considered, thus allowing for a better appreciation of the impact of an investment. For example, a filtering on 'investments in outreach/client relations' reveals expected returns in organizational competitiveness, which may be those expected by a firm, but also shows a strong link with the development of information-handling capacity in the client base. If this had not been considered, the perceived impact of the investment might have been skewed.

At present, the tool is best seen as an interactive summary of the connections made by our interviewees between investments in various aspects of IL and potential ROIs. The tool can become more comprehensive, and reflect a broader view, firstly by being used as the basis for investigations of IL practice in other enterprises, with data gathered from these used to refine and deepen the connections already displayed within. Another way to develop the research would be to use this initial framework to drive a more in-depth investigation of one or more enterprises, focused on seeking more specific and quantitative data on returns in specific organizational contexts over a period of time. Through doing so, a firmer estimate of the financial and other benefits of investment in IL, complementing and updating de Saulles' (2007) calculation, could begin to be made. But even before any further research is undertaken, the tool may be tested and deployed in business settings; users are encouraged to check its applicability and potential usefulness, and to provide feedback.

Conclusion

The DeVIL project has been a small-scale, preliminary investigation of how the value of IL to employers can be determined. The cases have helped to establish a range of areas in which a selection of enterprises are investing to promote IL among both their staff and their client/customer base; they have also identified areas of practice in which returns on these investments may accrue, directly or indirectly. This has enabled the creation of maps of the organizational areas in which returns on investments in IL can be expected. These are akin to 'base maps' of, say, urban areas over which further, quantitative information (say, levels of employment, or property prices) can later be overlaid. The DeVIL tool may be seen as a basis for subsequent investigations in specific contexts, and the beginning of a dialogue with businesses and any stakeholder interested in the use of information in employment contexts – through which the tool can be further refined.

The limitations of the project must be acknowledged, however, as these suggest areas in which further research might be directed. Firstly, these base maps have been constructed through data generated by a range of different stakeholders in three quite different organizations, and thus capture something of the potential variation in how the value of IL can be perceived (cf. Whitworth, 2014, 160–5). Missing, however, are the perceptions and views of other sorts of organizational players (e.g. large private sector businesses), and importantly, voices of 'on the ground' staff and the clients/customers: at best, the interviewees have acted as proxies for these perceptions. This does not invalidate our initial conclusions, but does show one way in which they can be further enhanced.

Owing to the context-specific nature of all information landscapes and, hence, all workplace IL practice, it would be an epistemological mistake to seek generic rules which can be applied without consideration for the unique features of given settings (Whitworth, 2014, 164–5). What has been created is an initial prototype *tool*, but like any tool, its relevance and effectiveness can only be judged *in practice*, undertaken by those on the ground. This chapter has attempted to summarize the broad *range* of factors that come into play when determining the value of IL to employers, but further research, in specific workplaces, will be needed in order to use these maps as the base for more context-specific data, and generally, to hone the tool and the insights which it provides.

CHAPTER 7

Information Literacy's role in workplace competence, 'best practice' and the ethics of professional obligation

Marc Forster

This chapter will discuss:

- how being information-literate in the workplace is to be ethical. The ethically information-literate employee seeks to develop their knowledge to a level which allows them to most effectively address the needs of patient, customer or client. Not to be information-literate may result in harmful outcomes.
- how this exhibits itself in IL's role in the achievement of competence, and beyond this in the quest for 'best practice': the most effective and efficient way to achieve the best outcome for patients or clients, based on all relevant information effectively analysed and integrated into the knowledge base.

Introduction

As is well known, IL is often ignored, or regarded as a preoccupation only of librarians, or something only relevant in academic settings. How can we persuade businesses and organizations, professionals and other workers of its necessity? In fact, IL has a particular key role to play in work life that is arguably more fundamental than any other discussed in this book: an ethical role.

This chapter discusses the idea of the *necessity* of IL in the workplace. That is, its *ethical* necessity, which is found in the requirement of professionals, indeed all employees, to operate at maximum effectiveness for the highest possible safety and benefit of customers, patients and clients (Forster, 2013). In the information-rich modern workplace, this effectiveness requires the optimum search/differentiation, critique and application of all relevant information. An ill-informed professional is a potentially incompetent, even dangerous, one. A professional who has failed to develop, or sought to develop and maintain, the ability to identify information lack, search for and identify all relevant information and critique it in order to maintain professional knowledge levels, and practises from that incomplete knowledge base, is practising unethically.

This is not a common way of looking at IL's role and value. However, there is little question that its wider adoption and promotion by librarians would further strengthen its profile, and help increase an awareness of its proper value in the workplace.

Awareness of Information Literacy's vital role

This chapter's origins can be traced to something unexpected in the IL experiences of a representative sample of professional workers. Some of the data from a research study (Forster, 2015a) discussed in earlier chapters suggested that IL may have a dimension not previously identified. This seemed to be related to its vital role in the fulfilment of the obligation to give the best possible care for patients. An information-illiterate nurse, due to her inability to operate from a full awareness of research evidence and other key information, risks patients' safety and well-being.

The question arose: could this reflect something significant about IL in the workplace as a whole? Implications drawn from professional and workplace theories of best practice, when added to those from research, did suggest that there was a wider significance; a significance that implied a higher value to Information Literacy than even information professionals are prone to give.

An uncommon perspective

Although IL is often discussed in the context of ethical use of information, and information professionals are aware of the significance of Evidence-based Practice (e.g. Evidence Based Library and Information Practice (EBLIP) conferences), the ethical *value* of IL is only rarely discussed in the professional literature – even in an oblique way. Lombard (2010, 16) described the role of IL in certain fields such as business and medicine, hinting that there is a certain 'morality' dimension in the sufficient and inadequate, correct and incorrect, search and application of information in such fields. Brody (2008) coined the concept 'information naïveté': the unfounded belief that one's information skills are up to the job in hand, and therefore one has obtained all relevant information and is therefore operating with full 'knowledge'. The situations which arise from information naïveté, in those professionals whose actions have significant consequences for others, are ethical. Ethical failure is located here in those individuals taking action based on inadequate or inappropriate information due to inadequate searching, critique or application, and by extension in the failure to properly consider the likelihood or significance of a personal deficit. Although most information naïveté has trivial consequences, in some contexts it can be fatal (Brody, 2008, 1127). An improvement in IL could solve or mitigate the problem. The information-literate person's awareness of information deficiency would imply that naïveté would be addressed.

It is perhaps a symptom of how IL has been 'ghettoized' within academic contexts, ones in which defects in effective information use have merely an academic rather than a 'real-life' consequence, that the actual danger of harm posed in workplace situations by the information-illiterate hasn't been fully acknowledged.

A research study's unexpected findings

A number of participants in the nursing study (Forster, 2015a) emphasized that not to make the greatest possible efforts to locate all of the information, and critique and apply all relevant research evidence appropriate to the patient's condition and relevant to the most effective methods of care, was to be irresponsible. Indeed, if you didn't have those information skills, you should be obliged to obtain them:

> . . . through necessity I have to follow Evidence-based Practice. It's an ethical
> issue.   Participant 3

> . . . most patients are vulnerable, are in a compromised situation – this is why
> you need ethics, accountability . . . and Evidence-based Practice to show that they
> are safeguarded.   Participant 3

> Patient safety is fundamental – everything that we do to them can be detrimental
> . . . we do have to keep up to date because everything we do [should be] based on
> sound evidence.   Participant 1

> If you say it's evidence-based you have the moral high ground. It's not just me –
> we have to do it   Participant 5

> . . . it would be unethical not to keep up with your [information skills], but I
> think with the best will in the world you're always going to have the movers and
> shakers and the people who follow behind.   Participant 36

I think as a Registered General Nurse – as a nurse – I owe it to my patients to be doing the best for them, which means [obtaining the] most up-to-date [evidence]. And I would feel that I was not doing my job – which I suppose is unethical . . . [and] you can't be giving old information out to patients because that could ruin their lives.   Participant 19

Evidence-based Practice – people need to really understand not just that it's a term but actually the way that they engage with Evidence-based Practice [including how they develop and use Information skills] has far-reaching effects and . . . has ethical implications   Participant 35

Once you've built up a repertoire of available evidence . . . it improves the patient's experience because what they're getting is not a one-size-fits-all approach. They are getting something which is literally tailored to their particular set of circumstances from people who are thinking and enquiring.
                                                                        Participant 7

They often used the terms 'ethical' or 'ethically', or implied an ethical context, when discussing how information skills – the finding, critiquing and applying of research evidence – were fundamental to making correct decisions about the most appropriate care for patients. This was particularly emphasized in critical care environments where operating without a basis in research evidence was to risk an outcome that was likely to be very serious for the patient. Evidence-based Practice was seen by most nurses as being an ethical responsibility; they were frequently aware that it required IL (however they label it) and that the latter is something a nurse must achieve. Details of the identification of information need, the searching, critiquing and applying of information were mentioned as significant and essential for Evidence-based Practice to be effective.

Those in senior positions, especially, understood that IL cannot be written off as something needed for study but nothing to do with real practice – an attitude still to be found in inexperienced nurses. Nor is it something a nurse, especially one of many years' standing, who did their training in the 'pre-IT age', can be excused from developing as something difficult and not sufficiently important for the effort required. Health professionals are ethically obliged to be 'information, and especially research-based information, aware'.

After the data analysis process described in Chapter 2, an ethical dimension was visible in several of the Dimensions of Variation generated under Theme/Context No. 3, for example:

• exploring the parameters of compassionate care

- focusing on the nature of patient safety
- achieving optimum and so ethically defensible care.

A list of similar ethically focused dimensions from throughout the seven themes included:

- obtaining sufficient psycho-socio-cultural background knowledge on a patient
- developing a culture of accountability to patients
- being seen to be accountable for actions
- becoming a patient advocate
- attempting to improve individual outcomes
- attempting to 'improve my practice'
- following guidelines, protocols and policy documents
- matching evidence to a very specific clinical context or specific patient
- using evidence to prompt additional, more detailed questions
- keeping up to date with the current evidence relevant to your job
- developing up-to-date practice
- establishing knowledge of, and understanding of, current practice and associate issues
- showing competence in day-to-day work.

How can the descriptor 'ethical obligation to be information-literate' be used to contextualize some of these statements which don't necessarily use the word 'ethical'? All of these quotations and formulations, it can be asserted, imply ethical actions in that they are focused on finding and using information to achieve optimum care. Ethical practice implies moral imperatives that govern a person's behaviour. In IL in healthcare these establish the necessity of effectively identifying an information lack, and locating, critiquing and applying information within clinical and managerial practice to help achieve best possible care of the sick and to empower patients in their treatment choices. In other professions these imperatives might establish the necessity of using information to provide the best service or advice, or empower clients so that they have the best chance of making effective financial or legal decisions.

Returning to the nursing study data, the quotations set out above seem to imply there is in nursing:

- a focus on acquiring the necessary personal and clinical information to sensitively determine the needs of the patient
- a necessity to be accountable to patients and colleagues, in which IL provides the best possible knowledge contribution to the individual's care and the work of the team

- an ongoing striving for professional competence in which IL has a key role in maintaining sufficient knowledge levels
- an ethical requirement to effectively and comprehensively identify, locate and critique research and other evidence necessary to the investigation of the parameters and characteristics of the *best possible* care.

These can be summarized as: (1) the ethical requirement to achieve competence; but beyond this, (2) the ethical requirement to seek out and implement 'best practice'.

Could this be confirmed in a broader context: one applicable to a range of different professions?

- Does IL take on an 'ethical' colouring, *by definition*, in professions which have an obligation to patients, customers or clients to perform in a *competent* manner? And if so, how?
- Is that colouring even more marked in those professions that demand the highest possible level of practice, through the location and analysis of research evidence into practice outcomes, in order to do the *very best* for those that rely on their service to protect and advise them?

The next section attempts to answer these questions.

A broader context: professional competence and 'best practice'

Evetts (2006) defines professionals as people who work in knowledge-based service occupations. Although some knowledge is obtained through further training, much has to be acquired 'on the job' and in the form of research evidence, guidelines and legal precedents (Forster, 2015a), and 'undocumented' information from colleagues and team members (Lloyd, 2010).

Many professions, and those who work in them, have the ability to alter the financial, medical, social or legal parameters of people's lives in the profoundest way, even to the extent of influencing whether a life continues. They must also deal with the ethical dimensions of the responsibilities that come with this power. A nurse, lawyer, financial consultant or social worker can facilitate great improvements in the quality of a life, but may also damage it through faulty, inappropriate or out-of-date practice. This is acknowledged in relevant codes of professional conduct (e.g. Nursing and Midwifery Council, 2010; General Social Care Council, 2010). Such codes also attempt to make practitioners aware of their responsibility to practise ethically, not only in the sense of being competent and so avoiding malpractice, but by fulfilling the obligation to do the best for the patient or client at all times. This involves doing all that could have been done; following what has been determined – perhaps by research or statistical analysis – to be effective or the most effective procedures and practices. Failure to do this may involve not doing the most to make oneself aware of all of the salient facts, the key documents or research evidence, or failing to develop the skills and knowledge necessary to make use of that information; in other words, a failure to be information-literate. It also follows that librarians whose information-gathering and critiquing activities inform the decision-making processes of medical and legal professionals, amongst others, must also be competent and diligent or they may also risk contributing to negative personal outcomes.

Professional competence

The basic level of acceptable practice in the workplace is usually labelled 'competence'. What is IL's role in assuring competence and what are the ethical issues around competence that might help us understand IL's ethical role?

> Competence is the state of having the knowledge, judgement, skills, energy, experience and motivation required to respond adequately to the demands of one's professional responsibilities.
>
> Roach, 1992, 61

In this definition of what constitutes professional competence, knowledge is listed first, and there may be some claim for it as being the fundamental basis of competence. Judgement is impaired, skills may be unusable and energy misplaced without sufficient and appropriate knowledge and the IL that initiates the formation of that knowledge. Competence is about keeping knowledge up to date. This is not just a matter of training, which is intermittent and not necessarily an exact fit for a 'knowledge gap' when it is available. It implies that professionals must be information-literate so that current professional knowledge and practice is *constantly* sought out, comprehended and adhered to. Competence or 'fitness to practise' is mentioned in a range of professional codes of conduct, for example, for Social Workers:

> As a Social worker, you must be accountable for the quality of your work and take responsibility for maintaining and improving your knowledge
>
> General Social Care Council, 2010, 10

Solicitors must sign up to the Law Society's 'Continuing competence scheme' through which they are obliged to maintain the currency of their practice

(Law Society, 2016). Nurses are obliged to 'Provide a high standard of practice and care at all times' (Nursing and Midwifery Council, 2010); to do this they must 'use the best available evidence.'

> 35. You must deliver care based on the best available evidence or best practice
> 36. You must ensure any advice you give is evidence based if you are suggesting healthcare products or services.
>
> Nursing and Midwifery Council, 2010

The competence–knowledge–Information Literacy link is clear in each case.

A further definition of competence by Kitchener (2000) brings in the recognition of knowledge inadequacy:

> Being competent involves having the knowledge, skills and abilities to perform one's professional role, and the ability to recognize when one's knowledge . . . [is] inadequate and impaired.
>
> Kitchener, 2000, 156

But professionals are also autonomous individuals who have responsibility to move on from recognition of a problem in their practice to actively doing something about it. Evetts's (2006) definition of the professional as someone who works in knowledge-based service occupations implies that competence must involve awareness of knowledge lack and the ability to plan and execute an information search and to identify, locate and critique that information to create new knowledge. Not all 'knowledge' is based on documentary information sources (Lloyd, 2010). However Eraut (1994) considered the factors on which learning in professional practice relies and found 'publications' to be one of the three key ones.

The failure to develop and use IL to maintain competence has an ethical significance for all professionals, not just those who could potentially endanger the public by their incompetence. Undermining the work of colleagues and employers is a potential risk in any profession; failure, through operation from an incomplete or inappropriate information base, to provide value for money to clients, or to provide a service which they themselves rely on as correct and effective in the development of their own products and services, may result in breach of trust or harm in one form or another. In the nursing study, the 'team approach' to IL is something which emerged very strikingly, confirming research from other studies (e.g. Lloyd, 2006; O'Farrill, 2008). Groups within the nursing profession or groups which included other professionals (the 'multidisciplinary team') often worked together to maintain effective care and treatment by a joint effort to search for and critique relevant research or research-based documentation. Information Literacy was seen as a way of effectively contributing to the team and the work of other professional groups. Failure to do so, to undertake a role and not perform it based on the research evidence or other information relevant to that particular role in the team, potentially undermines the work of all, and the well-being of all of the patients or clients dealt with by the team.

Best practice and the use of research evidence

In many professions Evidence-based Practice has been accepted as a means of keeping competence levels as high as possible (Sackett et al., 1997). This involves integrating professional experience and research evidence of the best possible working methods with the information gathered about a patient or client, to determine what is likely to be the best way of fulfilling the client or patient's needs.

> Evidence-Based Practice describes a philosophy and process designed to forward effective use of professional judgment in integrating information regarding each client's unique characteristics, circumstances, preferences, actions, and external research findings.
>
> Gambrill, 2007, 449

Evidence-based Practice involves identifying, finding and applying research evidence – raw evidence or guidelines or other documents based on that evidence – as a means of discovering and implementing what has been proven to be safe, effective, but also the most effective, practice. Essential knowledge is seen, not just in what has been accumulated over a career but what, objectively, the research indicates is the best way to act. Evidence-based professions have bred a huge research effort into the best methods of practice, the best treatments and the effectiveness or otherwise of working patterns. Information Literacy is no longer merely accumulation of knowledge to do the job effectively, but a process of constantly improving practice based on new research evidence as it becomes available. Changing practice requires the ability to find and critique information sources drawn from research evidence and apply it to practice – creating a new way of working. Evidence-based Practice is seen as an ethical tool in the professions that deal with human health and welfare, not only to combat ill-informed practice but to combat harmful wider phenomena. Gambrill (2007) sets out in tabular format the 'Contributions of Evidence-Based Practice to Honoring Ethical Obligations' and under 'Help clients and avoid harm' she places: 'Encourage use of and facilitate access to practice and policy related research findings to maximize the likelihood of success and minimize the likelihood of harm' (Gambrill, 2007, 456). Under the ethical obligation to be competent is placed

'Possess knowledge of and effectively transmit up-to-date research findings regarding vital practice and policy questions' (457). 'Use', 'facilitate access', 'possess knowledge of' (i.e. identify, locate and critique, and 'transmit') are familiar terms from definitions of Information Literacy (SCONUL, 2011).

The role of Information Literacy

The professional requirements that are competence and Evidence-based Practice can only be achieved through a comprehensive awareness and application of all relevant information, so that the professional operates at the most knowledgeable level possible. The use of all appropriate and relevant information to develop purposeful actionable knowledge is fundamental to the professional activity and practice of lawyers, medical professionals, investors, academics and other 'information workers'. Failure to operate from sufficiency of knowledge, and allow the uninformed, or partially informed, legal brief, treatment plan, investment portfolio or university course to masquerade as the 'real thing' can be interpreted as an ethical failure. Information Literacy must be achieved for a professional to practice ethically; it safeguards knowledge development by functioning as guarantor that a professional will operate, and will seek to operate, with an adequate grasp of *actuality*. It's clear that information professionals have a profoundly important role in workplace practice and professional education.

Professional decisions must be made based on a sufficient understanding of motive; of history; of process; of error; of capability; of lack; of symptom and aetiology; and of subjective, objective and group 'need'. Information-literate professionals make their crucial decisions from a sufficient body of information relevant to these and other aspects of actuality, critiqued effectively. The result is the best possible chance of safe, ameliorative or even transformative outcome. In the latter context especially, IL has a key role; operating from the confidence and sound judgement due to a solid knowledge base, the imagination can soar and to good effect. Schooled and grounded in a thorough grasp of what has been and has not been done and the potentialities and limits of knowledge, the professional can more easily leap to what might be done, so that the client or patient's world is transformed for the better in ways never before considered.

Clearly, the aim of developing IL should be a central one in professional education, and for the same ethical reasons that correct behaviour is inculcated. Information Literacy, so often struggling to make itself acknowledged, has the potential to take centre stage when properly valued through awareness of the contexts described above. However, the literature in IL development, as has often been remarked (Aharony, 2010), is still primarily published by librarians for librarians. Even those professions that acknowledge that they are 'evidence-based' often neglect the importance of training of students in these skills. Smith and Presser (2005), in their paper discussing IL training for student lawyers, observe that because a whole range of key information-based activities such as legal reasoning, legal writing, adherence to copyright law, and avoidance of plagiarism are essential to the effective modern lawyer, widespread failure to be educated into competence in these activities results in failure to serve the needs of the client and of the law itself. Elsewhere there is the same awareness and the same lack of 'action':

> The rhetoric of Evidence based practice fails to recognize that it is the ability to source and process information – in other words, 'information literacy' – which is the key to EBP. It is important to stress that it is the ability of the nurse to pose a precise and answerable patient-focused question that will facilitate a more efficient search of the literature and eventual retrieval of documents which can be interrogated through critical appraisal.
>
> Glasper, 2011, 188

In most cases there is no development in information skills beyond basic undergraduate-level competence (Howe, 2012). Perhaps in such evidence-based professions as the law and nursing an accumulation of research evidence on IL's key role is the way forward – a 'critical mass' which is still some way off. IL's many contexts, such as those mentioned in this chapter, must be more thoroughly and widely investigated. What is the relationship between information capabilities and competence in law? What is the ethical consequence of the social work department with poor internet access?

Summary

Without adequate subjective knowledge the professional is less likely to reach the highest practice ideals that promise the best possible outcome for the client, patient or customer. IL empowers the professional to be constantly, effectively seeking and applying the necessary relevant information so that she or he is able to give a knowledgeable contribution; one functioning with awareness of all relevant research or other input. Fully informed, the professional can be sure they are giving the very best service possible. This is only possible through IL. Although training can fill large knowledge gaps, gaps are unlikely to be completely filled and are constantly contextually evolving. Hence the workplace professional is **ethically obliged to seek to become information-literate and to perform in the workplace in an information-literate manner** in the pursuit of that knowledge.

As we have seen, despite limited research and discussion of this aspect of IL's role in the workplace and in professional practice, there is enough in our understanding of the principles of professional competence and Evidence-based Practice, and evidence from research, to draw conclusions about IL's ethical role in the life-changing and life-sensitive professions. Making the fullest effort to operate from adequate knowledge (relevant information justifiably considered to be true (Floridi, 2010; Hoyt, Bailey and Yoshihashi, 2012)) would appear to be fundamental to ethical practice in the workplace. The information base from which the professional operates must be as complete as can be reasonably achieved, in the sense that an attempt has been made to search effectively for all relevant information, and critical analysis has been applied to all potentially relevant information sources found. It could be hypothesized that if not, so that the paradigm-shifting research study, the key legal document or statistical analysis is missing, it could mean a failure of 'knowledge' and so inadequate treatment, advice or representation. IL involves not only understanding how to rectify this but also being able to determine that there are information sources which have yet to be incorporated into the 'knowledge base'. The information-literate person will then 'gather, use, manage, synthesize and create information and data' (SCONUL, 2011) effectively to rectify this, so that true knowledge is the result.

Employers may imagine that somehow, in the contemporary world of easy access to information through the internet, all relevant information automatically finds its way to forming the basis of knowledgeable practice, and therefore education in information use and development of IL attributes are not necessary. The evidence and arguments that show that IL is central to the achievement of the 'best practice' that all employers and conscientious professional desire, and is therefore an ethical necessity in a wide range of professions, are powerful indicators of its value and the real risks to that practice of its lack. Librarians thus have a potential means to address stakeholder complacency, create a more appropriate place for their IL educational activities in professional education and training and potentially, therefore, contribute to a more confident, competent and innovative professional workforce – a contribution that leads to better, healthier, more productive lives for patients and clients.

This is an important perspective on IL, but one previously on the whole unacknowledged. Librarians and information scientists should be at the forefront of the campaign to make it more widely understood. However, the lack of a wide range of relevant studies suggests further research might contribute to its dissemination. Research into the ethics of IL in evidence-based or information-rich professions such as law, finance and social work might shed further light on the role of IL in achievement of 'best practice', and the issues which arise from its lack.

CHAPTER 8

Learning within for beyond: exploring a workplace Information Literacy design

Annemaree Lloyd

This chapter will discuss:

- how the intensification of work and creation of new ways of working can present librarians with challenges in terms of creating Information Literacy (IL) education that provides scaffolding for students' transitions into professional or vocational practice.
- how by addressing this need, librarians must balance students' transitions at both ends of the process – into higher education or vocational settings, and then into the workplace. This complexity requires a recasting of pedagogical practices to accommodate changes in the nature of work. With this in mind, common themes drawn from practice-based research are used to construct a conceptualization of workplace IL instruction.

Introduction

Modern workplaces are *fast* places, blending traditional and new versions of work and ways of working. The workplace is now characterized by rapid rates of change; seamless integration of technology; the broadening of networks; incorporation of social media, e-mail and other multimedia platforms; and the ability to work without propinquity (White, 2012). The need to accommodate change and to provide innovative responses to workplace challenges requires employees to continually update, extend and improve their capacity to understand their workplace information landscapes. The increasing messiness of the workplace results in the growth of formal and informal sources of information, which compounds the issue of workers being able to identify, locate and share 'quality information' (Martin, 2013). The implications of these changes are increased uncertainty about employer expectations of new workers, and the need to ensure that new workers have the capacity to demonstrate information resilience (Lloyd, 2013).

This chapter considers the teaching of IL practice in the light of the messiness created by rapid workplace changes and evolving ways of working. Themes which are common to a practice perspective and act as a scaffold to conceptualizing workplace IL instruction are described. A premise of this chapter is that current models and frameworks of IL do not adequately prepare students for workplace learning because they do not account for the preparatory nature of higher education or for the change in learning cultures that new graduates and novices face when they transition into the workplace.

Bodies of literature related to IL, practice-based learning, transition, and workplace learning inform this chapter, which is guided by the question: 'How do we prepare students to transition from preparatory contexts to the world of work?' This question should be of interest to librarians charged with the responsibility of supporting the development of graduate attributes because it emphasizes the importance of scaffolding IL across the trajectory of students' university learning experiences.

The concept of *literacies of information* is also introduced to highlight the foundational nature of IL, and the complexity and deictic nature of information and technologies that form part of the information landscape of the modern workplace. In this view, IL, as a way of knowing (Lloyd, 2003), is *enacted* through contemporary literacies practices such as digital literacy, media or analogue literacy and information-related activities and competencies, which are shaped and authorized by a particular site or context. This approach draws our attention to the construct of IL as it is conceptualized through practice. *Information resilience* (Lloyd, 2012; 2014) is also conceptualized in this chapter as an outcome of IL practice and an attribute of an information-literate person. Information resilience describes the capacity to respond to uncertainty by learning to operationalize information skills and activities to gain access to information resources.

Finally, the chapter describes the DASIL model (Dimensions, Activities and Skills of IL) as a scaffold for developing IL instruction. The final section of this chapter considers IL in relation to building information-resilient workers.

Workplace Information Literacy research

A review of the corpus of literature for this topic will not be undertaken here (see the annotated bibliography by Lloyd, 2010; Williams, Cooper and Wavell, 2014). It is sufficient to note that workplace IL has not received the same attention from library and information studies researchers (Crawford and Irving, 2009; Head, 2012; Lloyd, 2010) as it has in other contexts. In many cases, research has been limited to understanding searching skills or to use with technology, with few studies exploring the deeper, complex nexus of working (i.e. working practices, performance and information creation and use). This means that IL researchers who are interested in the workplace must often draw from research that is conducted in other fields and that is relevant to understanding how people experience and use information in learning about work. In fields such as organizational studies and workplace learning, research into new versions of work (e.g. work that is hybridized, mobile or without spatial or temporal propinquity) can inform the pedagogical practices of vocational and university librarians. From an information perspective this kind of research can raise questions about the nature of information practices in the changing versions of work. It can also lead to questions about whether IL education taught in the preparatory contexts of university, school-based or vocational education has currency and relevance to the changing spatial arrangements of work and ways of working, e.g. project-based, or where workers need to navigate multiple contexts across a number of companies (Costas, 2013) or mobile work without the support of colleagues, established structures or the contingent sources of knowledge offered by traditional offices (Harmer and Pauleen, 2012). Head's (2012) research suggests that while students enter the workplace with an excellent ability to search for information online, they are often unaware of other sources of information that are necessary for the performance of work. Research by Central New York University (Gashirpv and Matsuucki, 2013) has identified that universities and academics need to pay more attention to what employers are saying – namely that, while students may leave formal education with an ability to use computers, they are lacking in the critical literacies of information that enable them to think creatively in order to find solutions to real-world problems that do not always involve finding the solution online. Similarly, White (2012), exploring work in the digital workplace, has indicated the need to be aware of how searching on different devices may produce different versions of the same result because of platform or language variations. These findings have implications for revisiting or recasting IL education.

Information intensification and new versions of work

Graduates enter a working world that has been shaped by the demands of new capitalism (Sennett, 2007) from which the knowledge economy has emerged. New paradigms of work are characterized by an intensification of workload and new versions of work may be mobile and cross boundaries (Costas, 2013), occurring in stable offices, but also out into temporary settings such as in cafés or airport transit lounges. This type of work requires workers to become agile critical thinkers, not only about the issues and challenges specific to work, but also those associated with the actual process of working. It also creates a paradigm shift where new versions of work are characterized by the increased availability of information; broader networks; a diversification of information sources; deictic forms of new media; a shift in flows of knowledge; a wider range of information access and output points; and changes in the temporal and spatial nature of the workplace, and in technologies used in the performance of work.

Achieving a high level of competitiveness requires organizations to reorganize themselves horizontally, to allow problem solving and decision making to flow laterally across the organization rather than vertically from the top (Baralou and Tsoukas, 2015; White, 2012). As a consequence, the information environments and landscapes of modern workplaces have become messy and highly complex, and the need to access and use information, to think critically, to become informed, and to create and innovate, has become a pervasive aspect of everyday working life.

Coupled with this, workers must become adept at information work, not only in relation to developing content knowledge, but also competency knowledge and expertise in managing the process and flow of work and use of technologies to ensure that workflow information remains uninterrupted by technology failures or service failures (Martin, 2013).

To accommodate the complexity of the workplace, new literacies of information have emerged alongside older and more stable literacies that support the multimodal workplace landscapes that workers experience. The intensification of the information environments of work influences the way an information landscape is experienced as a 'push and pull' environment. In addition to receiving information, workers now play a dynamic role as creators and evaluators, circulators and disseminators. The transition into professional practice is marked, first by the need to apply newly gained professional content knowledge in the performance of work, and second by the need to map the workplace environments and landscapes to understand their structural aspects and to recognize information affordances, and to connect with information sources about governance, work structures and sites of professional knowledge (Fenwick, 2013).

Current models of Information Literacy

At present, there is no model, set of standards or framework specifically related to workplace IL. Current models of IL are drawn from educational contexts, which in turn influence pedagogical thinking and instructional practices (ACRL, 2000; 2015; SCONUL, 2011; Secker and Coonan, 2011). In a review of these frameworks, standards and guidelines, Martin (2013) suggests that a more socio-cultural understanding of information has begun to emerge in these models as they are revised. According to Martin, IL is recognized as 'holistic, contextual and emerging out of an individual's information experiences' (Martin, 2013, 124). In all models, individual agency continues be highlighted, underpinning the focus on individual learners – bounded within educational structures.

Still missing, however, is serious consideration of the role of the community and other forms of knowledge and knowing that shape the contextual elements which form the information landscape and the information practices related to it (Harris, 2008; Lloyd, 2006). The absence of these elements from IL education continues to have implications for the development of reflective thinking, which is a critical element of IL practice, and one that is developed over time and in relation to the context or setting. It also has implications for students' IL development by confining and shaping their IL experience within the boundaries of educational practice.

In the UK, Secker and Coonan (2011) argued that IL still suffers from the disjuncture that exists between aspiration statements of IL as a critical catalyst to the complex learning required in the 21st century and integrated institutional frameworks, which place IL at the centre of discipline-based teaching and learning strategies. This has resulted in 'a failure to establish common frameworks and terminology and understanding around IL and what it is intended to achieve' (Secker and Coonan, 2011, 5).

In the USA, the Association of College and Research Librarians (ACRL, 2014; 2015) has finalized the *Framework for Information Literacy for Higher Education*. There is some evidence that the guidelines move away from a systematic concept of IL towards understanding IL as part of a 'complex ecosystem' akin to the information landscape construct (Lloyd, 2006).

In the framework, there is also a change in focus from textual objects as primary learning objects towards recognizing a recognition of a wider range of modalities (social, corporeal, in addition to textual) and the multimodal nature of literacies (visual, data, multimedia), which requires a broader range of metacompetencies (Lloyd, 2003). This appears to incorporate a genuflection to the social theory-based research of authors such as Lloyd (2010), Lundh and Alexandersson (2012), Pilerot (2016) and Limberg and Sundin (2006), who have identified the limitations of the previous skills- and individual-attribute-focused guidelines, and in doing so argued for conceptions that highlight the social and relational nature of the practice (ACRL, 2014, 4). This earlier research led Lloyd to state that IL had different contexts, different concepts and different truths (Lloyd, 2005).

In moving away from a fixed notion of IL, the framework advocates core understandings, sets of practices, ways of thinking, metacognitive strategies and critical reflection (ACRL, 2014, 4). While this approach provides a more realistic understanding of the role of IL in supporting ways of knowing (Lloyd, 2003), the terminology around the framework implies a rigid or bounded interpretation. This limitation may be a result of the document's inability to account for transition, and the role of preparatory settings – such as higher education institutions – to support the move from novice to expert to novice as individuals move through the higher education system, gaining expertise in the educational setting, but then requiring support to prepare for the novice state that will occur with transition to the workplace.

A changing perspective on Information Literacy: literacies of information

In some cases, the revisions to the current crop of frameworks acknowledge the deictic nature of new literacy practices and a more socio-cultural view of information. This change in perspective has resulted in IL practice often being renamed and rebadged. This is due to changes to information environments that are brought about by the exponential growth of knowledge and changes to information and communication technologies that are continually shaping and reshaping the way in which the practice is conceived (e.g. digital literacy, media literacy, computer literacy; the context of the practice, e.g. health literacy, academic research literacy; or the outcomes of the practice). Meanwhile, other iterations such as transliteracy emphasize the cognitive and social capabilities in communication across a wide range of contemporary literacies and media platforms (Andretta, 2009).

However, the foundational concepts related to IL as a practice composed of a range of activities and skills remain deeply lodged within each renaming. With each definition or rebadging largely focused on access to information, a more complex suite of literacies and multimodalities and material practices emerge. This complexity can be conceptualized as a *literacies of* information (first mentioned by Poirier and Robinson, 2014); the term reflects a more holistic way of thinking about the many activities and skills that are enacted in context, and which act as a conduit between people and information.

How we know is reflected through the dimensions of our social contexts. As a practice, IL is inherent within other practices, particularly learning. Consequently, it is difficult to talk about learning without acknowledging that *information* is central to all learning. This single point is important, as it has implications for how we teach IL and what elements we focus on at the higher education and vocational levels. A changing view from IL to include the companion concept of literacies of information is closely aligned with the common features of the practice approach – specifically as practices such as IL are shaped by the social-political, material-economic and cultural-discursive dimensions (Kemmis and Grootenboer, 2008) that shape the 'site of the social' (Schatzki, 2002) and the material practices inherent within it.

Core workplace themes which influence a practice-based learning design

A number of practice-based themes (Gherardi, 2009a; Orlikowski, 2007; Schatzki, 2002) inform an evolving view of workplace IL and can contribute to developing workplace IL-focused pedagogy. These themes are situated within historical and social contexts, emphasizing the collective, relational and embodied nature of practice and ways of knowing in the workplace. The concepts of transition and travel are also important scaffolding elements which must be acknowledged. Each theme is briefly described in the next section.

Collective nature of work

Practices are composed of collective and situated processes (knowing-in-practice) that connect 'knowing, working, organising, learning and innovating' (Reich and Hager, 2014, 3). In previous studies of IL in the workplace (Bonner and Lloyd, 2011; Lloyd, 2009; 2010), the practices that shape and name work are viewed as collaborative enterprises between occupational knowledge and the institutional and technical discourses of a setting. The mediation of the information landscape through information sharing plays a significant role in workers developing a shared sense of practice, performance, context and content. A significant aspect of the collective nature of work emphasizes the tacit, nuanced and contingent forms of information that are only available at the moment of practice, yet shape those intersubjective understandings that allow teams to form.

Socio-materiality of work

Taking up this theme, Orlikowski (2007, 1437) argues that 'the social and material are considered to be inextricably related – there is no social that is not also material, and no material that is not also social'. Knowledge is therefore embodied and mediated through the signs, symbols and tools of practice (Lloyd, 2006). Embodied knowledge is produced through practice. This knowledge (know-how) is anchored in performance of practising from the situatedness of the practice and material objects, signs and symbols of practice. The theme of 'practical understanding' has been taken up by a number of authors. Gherardi (2009b, 354) suggests that knowledge is embodied and practices anchored through material practices.

Embodied nature of work

The physicality of practice that is located within the body is an important source of information about practical knowledge, but also about nuanced, contingent and often peripheral ways of knowing that are temporally and spatially situated. In discussing the relationship that exists between knowledge and practice, Gherardi (2009b, 354) suggests that 'not only do people work with bodies, they also know through them'. Schatzki (1996, 44) adopts a more ontological approach, locating the body as a central feature of practices, and indicates that 'it is through the performance of bodily actions that the performance of other actions is constituted or affected'. The embodied nature of work has been described previously (Lloyd, 2006; 2010), and understanding the corporeality of practice presents challenges for the development of workplace IL instruction whose traditional IL instructional roles have focused on student's access to print.

The relational nature of work

The relational nature of work refers to variety of relationships that exist amongst people who are connected to each other in the same practices (e.g. school librarians, teachers, school principals, administrators) and who share the same work endeavours and material objects (computers, machines, tools) (Reich and Hager, 2014, 424). Expanding on this theme, Reich and Hager suggest that 'practices are always co-produced by a range of actors in space and time with bodies as vital locus of the practice' (2014, 425).

Historical and social antecedents of work practices

Work practices have histories and are shaped and reshaped over time by institutional and social dimensions. Central to this idea is the role of power in the shaping of a work practice. Power can be located within the sanctioning and legitimizing of practice-based knowledges at formal (e.g. institutional) and informal (group) levels. The ideas of transition through practice and change over time are also suggestive of the temporality of practice, and need to be considered in IL learning design. The evolving and changing nature of work requires an agile and information-resilient workforce.

Transition

The concept of transition is taken up in this chapter, as it is connected to the construction and reconstruction of identity (learning to become a student; being a student; and then learning to become a practitioner). Transitions are fundamentally about learning and Fenwick (2013) identifies three main dimensions of transitions that affect professional work. These are described by Fenwick as:

1   regulation, governance and accountability – which references a need to understand organization control (new managerialism); compliance and adherence to regulations; regulation of performance; and increasing emphasis on customer choice, which contests professional knowledge.
2   professional work structures – interpersonal work requires collaboration between diverse groups of experts (e.g. multiagency). This shift blurs knowledge boundaries and may result in new ways of knowing professional knowledge domains.
3   ways knowledge is produced, reproduced and circulated within professional communities (Green, 2009, 4). According to Fenwick there is a distinction between 'practice-as-knowledge and knowing *per se*. Graduates require the capacity to perform work in ways that are guided by and validated against shared knowledge and established conventions for practice' (Fenwick, 2013, 356).

Foundational to these conceptions of transitions is the requirement to reduce uncertainty in relation to each by establishing transitional competency, which enables new graduates to enter the workplace work-ready.

A practice-based approach to teaching Information Literacy

The DASIL (Dimensions of Activity and Skills of Information Literacy) model emphasizes the dimensions of practice through which sayings and doings shape the activities and skills that emerge to connect people to the various information landscapes that constitute the knowledge base of the setting.

Practice-based approaches have the potential to inform a pedagogical model for IL. These approaches emphasize the relational elements of community and participation (Lave and Wenger, 1991), and enactment, which is shaped by the socio-cultural, material-economic, and cultural-discursive practices of the setting (Kemmis and Grootenboer, 2008; Reich and Hager, 2014). Shove, Pantzar and Watson suggest that a practice combines a bundle of elements that are enacted through meaning, competency and materiality, which form together and link together in specific ways (Shove, Pantzar and Watson, 2012).

Enacting a practice such as IL is therefore accomplished through ongoing relationships and interaction between people and the objects of their practice, where meaning (know-why – about the practice) and competency (practice know-how) combine with the material artefacts, signs and symbols of the practice (technologies, tools and texts). A practice-based approach to IL education is antithetical to cognitivist or behavioural approaches because it does not position learning as an acquisition rooted in conceptions of technical or instrumental rationality; nor does it advocate for an individual epistemology of practice.

Information literacy is inherently entwined with other social practices and is shaped in the same way as other practices, reflecting the socio-cultural, material-economic and cultural-discursive practices of the setting (Kemmis and Grootenboer, 2008). To become information-literate and to know the information landscape and its paths, nodes and edges requires understanding how the normative and non-normative modalities of information are legitimized within a setting. Therefore, it is important that in developing a practice-based approach to workplace IL pedagogy, librarians accommodate skills and activities that enable students to engage with:

- meaning – what knowledges are legitimized within a setting; what performances are legitimized?
- competencies – the skills and know-how that are operationalized in the practice
- materiality – the range of technologies and artefacts through which the practice emerges and is enacted   (Shove, Pantzar and Watson, 2012).

A practice-based approach to teaching IL also requires that students develop a broader and more holistic approach to understanding how information travels within the workplace. A holistic approach suggests that students develop the capacity to recognize:

- **Dimensions:** these are the social conditions that influence and shape what knowledges are sanctioned and what ways of knowing are enabled or contested. These social dimensions represent power and control over how information and sites of knowledge and information practices emerge. Identifying the dimensions that influence IL practice, allows students to recognize which literacies of information enable or constrain ways of knowing (digital, visual, corporeal, media, etc.).
- **Activities and skills of information work:** these relate to information work (e.g. critical thinking, information seeking, searching, sharing) and application of skills (e.g. finding, defining, accessing) representing the performance of IL practice (e.g. the way in which information is created, produced, reproduced, circulated, disseminated and accessed, how information is sought and managed relative to the dimensions of the setting or context).

Becoming information-literate is characterized by transitions from unknowing to knowing. This transition occurs on many levels creating many types of information landscapes (workplace, education, etc.) that represent the myriad practices that constitute social life (Schatzki, 2002). The transitions occur in relation to knowledge domains but also in relation to subjective and intersubjective agencies.

The DASIL model is represented in Figure 8.1.

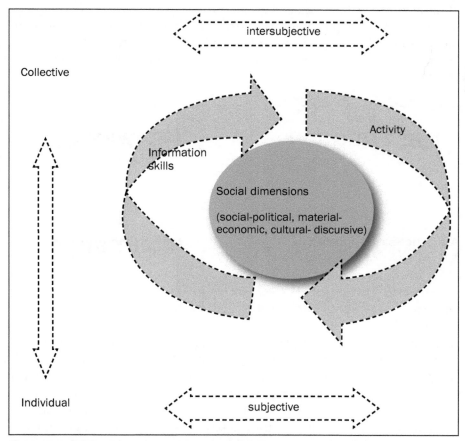

Figure 8.1 *DASIL (Dimensions of Activity and Skills of Information Literacy: a practice-based model)*

Conceptualizing Information Literacy learning design

Despite all good intentions, in general the teaching of IL and the development of IL programmes have a tendency to fall back on the most common and easiest of denominators – a focus on library-derived information skills – and at a minimum the bolting-on of IL as end-on sessions related to either library- or discipline-based orientation. This approach does not allow the scaffolding required to engage students to disciplinary or competency knowledge of the workplace.

The approach explored in this chapter suggests that IL has a trajectory, continually moving from stages of unknowing to knowing, i.e. from novice to expert, in the context of spatial and temporal dimensions (Figure 8.2). Consequently, the process of teaching IL necessitates that educational librarians extend their understanding of IL and the nature of workplace learning and develop new forms of strategic knowledge that accommodate the multimodal nature of information work and new versions of work. The learning design offered here mirrors the movement from novice to expert to novice.

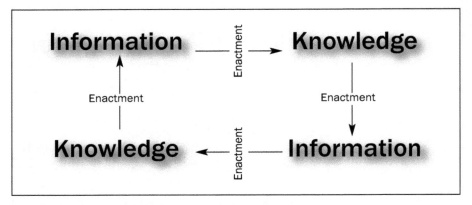

Figure 8.2 *Enactment of Information Literacy practice (adapted from Lloyd, 2004, 173)*

A learning design for IL in vocation and higher education sectors should accommodate the students' capacity to connect with the practice through competences, material and meanings (Shove, Pantzar and Watson, 2012) taking into account the preparatory nature of the setting and the trajectory of student movement from entry to exit. At the entry phase, the initial need is student engagement with abstract discipline-based knowledge and the corresponding IL practice that is associated with accessing information within this epistemic community. The exit phase focuses on the final stages of education, which should be geared to preparation for transition into the first year of work.

Information literacy therefore requires a programme of study which targets the various stages of the student educational experience and focuses on developing competencies that will enable graduates to draw from knowledge about IL practice to allow its enactment in workplace performance. The one-size-fits-all approach is not relevant to, nor is it suitable for, practice-based IL education.

To accommodate the preparatory and transitionary elements of higher education or vocational settings the IL programme requires three stages. Each stage corresponds to the student learning trajectory, taking into account the practice elements of meaning, competency and materiality (Shove, Pantzar and Watson, 2012), described in an earlier section of this chapter.

A significant feature of a practice-based approach to IL education is a focus on constructive alignment, which is woven through each phase. Developing effective IL practice requires that tasks, learning and teaching experiences are connected and aligned to the objectives related to IL practice development in the context of the discipline in the first phases and then of professional practices as students begin the transition phase.

Constructive alignment is defined by Briggs (2003, 27) in the following way: 'the "constructive" aspect refers to what the learner does, which is to construct meaning through relevant learning activities. The "alignment" aspect refers to what the teacher does, which is to set up a learning environment that supports the learning activities appropriate to achieving the desired learning outcomes.'

Stages of Information Literacy development

While not prescriptive, a practice-based programme would accommodate the following stages.

Preparatory stages

Learning performance relates strongly to engaging with abstract discipline-based knowledge (know-why knowledges), and to learning the performance of IL as an enactment of higher education or vocational discourse. In the preparatory stages, student focus is on becoming embodied in the learning practice of the higher education institution through engagement with the epistemic and instrumental knowledges related to rules and regulations, and to undertake activities that connect students with the meaning making that is required to connect with their specific disciplines:

- **meaning:** enabling students to connect to the symbolic and practical meanings associated with engagement with discipline knowledge and with the discourse and discursive practices which shape the University
- **competency:** related to shaping of IL practice (activities and skills) in relation to the sayings, doings and relatings (Kemmis and Grootenboer, 2008) of the setting (discourse and discursive practice)
- **materiality:** the technologies that support literacies of information in the setting.

Evidence from the workplace literature suggests that reflective practice is context-bound (Smith and Trede, 2013), so the focus should be on the higher education context, more abstract-discipline knowledge base. Reflective practice should be introduced in the preparatory stage and focused towards understanding IL in the context of educational practices and the student's experiences of IL in the higher education/vocational setting.

Information Literacy emerges as embedded IL classes, coupled with disciplinary knowledge related understanding, the context of learning, and ways of knowing within the context. Introduction to critical IL skills should also include introduction to discourses and discursive practices related to university or vocational learning.

Intermediate stages

Emphasis at this stage is on continued development of critical skills (i.e. critical evaluation of information, problem solving and reflection on practice focusing on understanding information-seeking practices, conceptualizing information practices in the context of the discipline- or competency-based approach). Information Literacy emerges as:

- **meaning:** the ability to understand the shape of the learning environment and specific discipline and what enables and constrains information creation, reproduction, circulation, dissemination
- **competency:** competency in engaging with a range of activities that facilitate access to disciplinary knowledge
- **materiality:** the technologies and activities that support literacies of information in the setting.

Transition to work stage

The final stages of tertiary or vocational study are geared towards the transition to work and professional or vocational practice. In this phase, students must move beyond abstract discipline-based understanding of work towards more situated understandings of IL practices at work.

At this stage, librarians must refocus their attention away from the library and towards the transition to work experience. Therefore, a climate that will facilitate transition should be constructed, considering elements of authentic practice and problem solving, affording the opportunity for some generic elements of the practice (e.g. general internet searching and evaluating skills) to travel in ways that may be relevant and support the students as they begin the process of learning about the information landscapes of work and the literacies of information that support ways of knowing.

In this stage, the focus shifts to developing practice competency that can be enacted in workplace settings, allowing students to enter new information landscapes, with the ability to adapt to the range of literacies of information that support the work of the setting. Drawing from disciplinary and practice-based knowledge (which may be gained through visits to workplaces, or by surveying students who return from work placements) activities should be related to authentic practice, such as collaboration, reflection on action and practice that reflect situated everyday practices, bearing in mind that nuances related to social modalities will not be accessible but should nonetheless be acknowledged in the programme (Brown, Collins and Duguid, 1989; Herrington, 2006).

During this transition stage, students need to connect know-why knowledge with know-how (Lloyd, 2006). This requires reflection on:

- **meaning:** connected to the symbolic and practical meanings associated with engagement with discipline knowledge and with the discourse and discursive practices that may be encountered in the first year of work
- **competency:** related to shaping of IL practice (activities and skills) in relation to the sayings, doings and relational dynamics of the setting (discourse and discursive practice)
- **materiality:** the technologies that support literacies of information in the setting.

Building resilience for workplace transition: the role of librarians

A practice-based design addresses the teaching and learning of IL as central to learning and an important graduate attribute. Teaching the practice of IL at tertiary levels requires that librarians develop a resonance with the workplace and view their role not as pushers of information but as translators, mediators, sources of knowledge and collaborators:

- **Translators:** Librarians need to have knowledge about disciplinary information practices, and ways of knowing how disciplinary landscapes are constructed and the types of literacies of information that enable or constrain access.
- **Mediators:** Librarians are placed in unique positions to mediate the educational and discipline/workplace landscapes in order to identify knowledge, competencies and skills that students will require while studying and when in transition to the workplace.
- **Source experts:** This refers to the expertise of librarians in understanding the role of information and knowledge from both a disciplinary and a competence perspective.

- **Collaborators:** with employers, trainers, other educators and students who undertake practical work or work placements.

The framework described here emphasizes the phases which should be conceptualized in the construction of workplace IL programmes. Underpinning this approach to IL education design is the incremental development of knowledge – about IL as a practice and a metacompetency (Lloyd, 2003) that facilitates ways of knowing about content and the various literacies of information that will be enacted.

The process of moving from a preparatory setting into the workplace can be fraught with difficulties, as educational landscapes fracture and new workplace landscapes emerge. A key to addressing the uncertainty of transition is the information resilience that can be claimed as an outcome of IL practice. A key to reducing uncertainty is the capacity to connect and engage with information to solve problems associated with entering new or unfamiliar settings or adapting to changed situations (Lloyd, 2013). Herein lies a central role for university and vocational education librarians. The challenge is to consider how new versions of IL pedagogy and instruction practices might also be recast to accommodate old and new versions of work and working.

Conclusion

An important lesson emerging from workplace IL research (Head, 2012; Lloyd, 2010) is that, in IL, the practice does not stand alone from the many practices that create and construct a context. Rather, IL is a practice that is dispersed within a practice and is central to its construction. A practice-based approach to IL embraces the notion that practice (including workplace learning) is social. Therefore teaching IL is not simply about skills but also about developing the critical thinking and problem-solving skills that use access to information as the catalyst for motivated and purposeful action. These elements are critical to workplace learning.

This will require different ways of thinking, but if taken up could open up a new area and new opportunities for librarians in academic and vocational settings to support learning 'from within for beyond'.

CHAPTER 9

Developing information professional competences in disciplinary domains: a challenge for higher education

Stephen Roberts

This chapter will discuss:

- the ways in which higher orders of information professional competence, including Information Literacy (IL), can be introduced into programmes of higher education teaching and learning.
- how such an approach to information professional education can lead to a deeper and wider dissemination across workplace occupations and domains, and see these competences embedded in organizational learning and personal development.

Introduction

Information Literacy is the child of an age when there was a clear and purposeful link between physical documents as the primary stores of recorded information and libraries and other physical locations as repositories. The principles and practices of librarianship provided the main means of management of content and access. For all the detail and complexity that lay behind this relationship, the user, in any form and from any perspective, was presented with a straightforward and largely linear model of access and use. Information Literacy could be constructed on the premise that a map of the bibliographical terrain could be perceived, tools designed to provide access and means found to obtain what the user needed. Not quite a one-dimensional environment but one in which a clear underlying logic could be presented to help complete the information cycle from production to consumption. The search for information and the mastery of the tools to access it can be viewed as a two-dimensional spatial problem. Providing IL (as it is now called) – or its contemporary equivalents of 'reader advice' (pre-1960s),

'user education' (1960s), 'information skills' (1970s and 1980s) and 'information education' (from the 1990s onwards) – started with a default position
of a skill transfer from librarian or information professional to reader and
user. Some ideas of the substance and complexity of these issues have been
ably reviewed by Nigel Ford (Ford, 2004; 2008) and are carried forward by
fellow contributors to this collection.

However, the impetus was slowly changing from a librarian-centric view
towards the user-centric view. Making the goal a shift of power from librarian
or information professional to the user was very much in tune with
educational and pedagogical theory. The skilled and informed user would be
transformed into an independent learner and then be set on a path to
independent and critical thinking. In the late 1980s in the UK this logic was
embedded in reforms of primary and secondary education (the National
Curriculum) and librarians and schools attempted to move in step with each
other to deliver a change in stance. Higher education has tracked all these
changes over three decades not only to improve its own educational
performance but also to show or suggest a seamless linkage between the three
educational levels. Certainly, this has provided a reason for higher education
librarianship to innovate and to claim its relevance to the wider education
community. Add to the cocktail of 'independent learning' the demands of
addressing employability, challenging the relevance of higher education
versus professional education and apprenticeship/internship and there is a
justification for the logic behind the title of this chapter.

The theme of transferable skills has informed the discussion of IL at all
levels of education. In this chapter the focus is narrowed to higher education
and targets the links between tertiary education, transferable IL competences
(and associated higher learning competences) and employability, especially
within professional contexts. If this relationship can be constructively
demonstrated it will not only satisfy more restricted criteria of professional
competence and qualification but also provide a model for a wider diffusion
of a high order of informed citizenship. Pragmatically defined 'informed
citizenship' implies a citizen aware of information (and knowledge) as an
active source of enablement and enrichment, providing access to sustained
advantages in life work and leisure, quality of life and well-being in general.
Essentially such citizenship can be seen as a progressive, liberal and
egalitarian construct, which may be reinforced by a range of rights and
protocols envisaging a *de facto* or even *de jure* body of information law to
protect these values. The transfer and trickle down of the outcomes from these
processes of education, employability and wider citizenship opens up
perspectives of a significant order which are themes for continued debate.

Before proceeding with this exploration there has to be a note of caution.
There needs to be a critique and evaluation of the performance and impacts

of IL itself. Surely 'more research is required' but at the very least there has to be some consensus of the principles and theory upon which investigation is grounded. There is research evidence for improvement on the basis of 'experimental trials' but such evidence is not easy to follow up as in a cohort study. In addition, the environments of end-users and applicable technologies are themselves subject to dynamic changes. But at the very least we can observe the accretion of good practices and infer that these may contribute to a general rise in competence and transfer of skills to an ever wider range of tasks. The generally phenomenal growth and success of all new technologies from web browsing to social media should be grounds for optimism, provided its use is in an ethical and respectful framework. If there is a trend to welcome in the 'new' we need to also ensure that traditional skills and resources of the 'paper economy' are not lost. We need to be 'digital and literate', not just 'digitally literate'.

Today and inevitably continuing into the future, the environment is one of multi-dimensionality and possibly even parallel worlds in which the perspectives of information and literacy have broadened and within which new and fresh responses have become evident. The initial applications of computing to information processing, the evolution of IT as a product of the fusion of computing and telecommunications and latterly the development of the internet and web technologies has engendered the continuing digital revolution. The one/two-dimensional world of the tradition has been absorbed into movements of change and in the process has obtained gains at the input phase of the information and communication cycle (generate-search-retrieve) but the digital revolution has continued to rupture the singularity at all points of the same cycle.

So now the stores of recorded information run the full gamut from tangible and physical to digital, virtual and intangible across a variety of communication media (written, visual and audio). Physical repositories still maintain a strong and vital presence and are complemented and co-exist with digital repositories, which themselves are situated within a wider mesh of resources, events and evidences that inhabit the world wide web. The management of content and access has evolved so that the older order of catalogues, indexes and classifications has for many been supplanted by a world of metadata and search engines, which however innovative and novel are strongly related to underlying logic and principles of search and retrieval.

Thus the 'spatial map', real or imaginary, has been changed and the navigational tasks within IL have been altered, even deformed. On the premise that the older mapping was a useful basis for navigation, whether or not it was adopted and integrated by the user, we will continue to propose and even test whether the new mapping can shape navigation and become an important component of an emergent and well aligned IL. In many ways the user remains a constant, even if the landscape continues to change. The most obvious changes to the landscape of IL and information have little to do with the 'old' and everything to do with the 'new' of technology and its impact on people, behaviour and society. The new IL is increasingly profiled in an emergent socio-technical system. Mobile telecommunications and mobile platforms, multimedia, the social media and social and behavioural changes are forceful, effective and radically different.

If the user remains a constant, the characteristics and behaviours of users (and non-users) are varied and evolving and often unpredictable. These features have to be accepted at face value, but do not imply the lack of a model to provide a template for defining and assisting behaviour. The user inherits an innate capacity to learn as a characteristic of our species and it is this which can provide the means to adjust to the changing environment and landscape of information. The substance of this chapter is thus to address these questions at the level of higher education, which provides the stepping stone to employability and professional and personal fulfilment. Any way in which IL can enhance these determinants of life chances has to be made seriously visible.

Foundations and assumptions: past, present, future

What baseline can be identified in IL in secondary and tertiary education in order to build a new practice? In spite of some two decades of reform, at least in the UK secondary-to-tertiary transition, there is little certainty that first-year undergraduates bring with them a coherent body of knowledge and technique that can guarantee a fast adaptation to new study conditions, and to the professional life that hopefully lies beyond. Almost invariably first-year courses have increasingly made play of the need to revise and embed not only library and information skills, but study skills more generally. The battle to 'library educate' and make entrants to higher education 'information-literate' has largely been lost. The majority conform to the stereotype of the Google generation (Nicholas and Rowlands, 2008). This is no surprise after a period of dis-investment in school libraries and the coincidental run-down of a public library tradition. A picture is literally more valuable than an engagement with a thousand words. Those who persevered in this tradition may still become the library and information workers of the future, but are never likely to be cloned to provide for the needs of an information-informed citizenship of the anticipated future.

Let us then be mildly radical and say that the current status quo is not going to continue for the informed citizen of the anticipated future. Will these citizens lack power as such if they do not master the realms of information and knowledge? A systematic improvement in IL is not likely to be a short cut to a solution. However, 'newer' concepts of relevance and motivation are likely to play a stronger part and may form a much better trigger for IL. If the Google generation shares the illusion that immediacy, serendipity and ease of use are inherent in their environment they may yet find a way to become information-informed. Diversity of content, intermeshing networks and volatility may provide a route to the satisfaction of information needs. On the other hand, simply increasing exposure to channels and redundancy might equally be a route to improvement. To understand the cognitive maps of these clients (however interesting to specialists) may not be such a necessity. Let us then assume that an information design-led provision may be a better investment than individual investment in IL up to a certain point. The motivation to persist and explore may be the most valuable personal asset. This motivation might lead to realization that if the resource system is designed, or even partially designed, the satisfaction of information needs may be achieved.

In this emergent model the provision of routes into the system could be the solution to discovery. The power may shift to the designers in the first place, so that the users ultimately discover their own power and capacity through interaction with the system. The model is never going to be one of deliberately arming the user, but more likely one of creating motivation and 'nudging' the user towards routes of satisfaction. This model may have the effect of increasing the power and status of information professionals, if such was their concern! But the real engine for the system possibly lies in a combination of the back room developing and innovating, and motivated use to reveal what is required from the system. This could ensure an outcome that the end-user is both satisfied and empowered.

Essentially this is the contemporary metaphor. A search engine works to deliver results but the user does not need to know how the work is done (but if they are curious they may ask and find out!) It is the design of the system that is crucial and critical. This argument works for both old technologies and for the new. A good physical library may contain what is needed for satisfaction but the user needs to know how to use the system to release the value. The world wide web can handle equally diverse content in digital stores and has to provide the tools and engines to extract the content.

On this basis, that system design is at least as important as user skill and competence, the purpose of (professional) IL is to provide mapping tools and processes as much as extractive tools. To this end the PIIK model (revealed in the following discussion) can be tested to provide foundations for a sufficient mapping to link user motivation and purpose to the world of information resources.

The challenge: developing highly information-literate professionals

The term 'information professional' (IP) attained currency in the UK during the 1990s after a protracted but necessary debate about the future of our professional associations and responses to change in the library and information sector and to a strategic reflection on identity and image within the occupational sector. The term (IP) has come to provide an umbrella expression to denote the recognized educational and occupational focus for the qualified librarian, information manager, information services provider or knowledge manager, and for those who work in the fields of documentation, records and archives. It has become a term to reflect the rise of an information-intensive society and the knowledge economy based not just on ICT and digital platforms but on wider social, behavioural and organizational changes to which these are linked. With a professional group so defined there is not only an aspiration to engender a wider dispersion of higher-order professional competences in information and knowledge work but a real possibility to propagate such roles and capacities more widely across other occupations and social groups.

Building an informed citizenship with these competences is a challenge still to be met in full. As a starting point, the writer revisits an initiative undertaken during the development of an MSc in Corporate Communication at the University of West London (UWL). An opportunity was identified in this information- and communication-rich discipline for information-professional academics to make an innovative contribution to a professional curriculum. A module was developed – 'Presenting Information Intelligence and Knowledge' (PIIK) – to provide a focus for introducing an information-professional contribution to curriculum and learning (Roberts, 2002; 2004). The module was favourably received by external assessors, examiners and industry professionals and students found it challenging and worthwhile. Thus, it may suggest a model for developing information professional competences in disciplinary domains. Some further personal validation of the spirit of the PIIK module was also explored in a much less obvious candidate area in the context of an MSc in Project Management, taught jointly in the School of Business. Further acquaintance with teaching in aviation management and IT and business undergraduate degrees (like the ITMB degrees) has provided the writer with more exposure to the issues in practice. To this can be added an information professional education experience on the UWL MA in Information Management in terms of a module entitled 'Information and Education', aiming to address the core issues of information learning for both educators and for information professionals. Professional practitioners will be able to relate the writer's experience to their own circumstances as librarians and/or educators.

The philosophy and purpose of PIIK was as follows (quoting from its module study guide):

The module takes the theories and practices of information management, organisational studies and behavioural science as leading tools and techniques for use in knowledge management as an integrated, hybrid and synergetic methodology which exploits information as a resource, facilitates organisational and individual decision making, and acknowledges the ways in which the resourcefulness of information produces and necessitates change in organisational and individual behaviour as goal fulfilment is sought.

The module will focus especially on the needs of (corporate communication) practitioners and assist the acquisition of practical concepts and techniques which can be used in organisational and individual practice.

The rationale for this module lies in the progressive evolution of information and communication activities in a global setting. Information systems, information management and information services provide the platform upon which the higher order range of knowledge-related activities are built. Students who have already studied these precursors will find the study and practice of knowledge management to be a natural progression in their intellectual and professional development.

The focus of the PIIK module was to build on a range of existing provision for information skills, learning skills and IL and competence in a professionally focused Master's course. This would provide reinforcement to areas in which the information professional community in education has already made an investment, for example in course inductions, ongoing assistance from subject specialist librarians and in increasingly user-facing and user-friendly library interfaces. The returns from this investment are still rather thin and insufficient: indeed, possibly disproportionate to the amount of effort made to develop programmes and embed competences. The investment needs to continue, but at the same time, a refreshed paradigm needs to be developed and appraised. This paradigm will seek a much stronger embedding of information professional competences in the different disciplinary domains. This chapter offers PIIK as a potential model for debate and as a means to stimulate further practice.

The PIIK model: a prototype for development
The module rationale

This chapter proposes a baseline for development of modules such as PIIK, exploring conceptual underpinnings and carrying out a review of the actual and potential scope for improvement, as well as how this could be translated and further generalized across other professional courses. For this discussion PIIK is used as both a vehicle for theory and for application to any professional practice. 'Theory' to provide the basis for directional as well as personal mappings of the information terrain (and potentially cognitive models of information processing and management) and for an experiential and developmental practice in the context of 'Application'. The realization of this aspect of theory and practice was considered by Levy and Roberts (2005) in a collection of essays published within the 'development cycle' of PIIK. Many of the contributors have continued to develop ideas and practices exposed at that time.

The PIIK model helped to explore the balance between *content* (awareness, location and appreciation) and *processes* both in terms of information handling and retrieval and the wider conspectus of information and communication behaviour. This suggests a model to support an informed and reflective professional, who can then apply the learned outcomes to personal workplace practice in the shorter term. In the longer term the model may work towards shaping policies and colleague behaviours to face up to and solve real problems and issues of any given professional and/or occupational domain and practice. The application of the model posits a growing sense of information awareness that can be a precursor to a developed information culture in a profession, domain and practice. This points towards a level of culture which can enable personal empowerment and information empower- ment which can really make a reality that information and knowledge is power gained from an inherent understanding of the value and impact of information and communication. In short, the PIIK approach may provide a stepping stone to information citizenship.

The PIIK model was developed around a 14-theme structure relevant to information and communication professional communities (Figure 9.1). Post- development reflection in the context of widening the application to other professional communities suggests the value of a 6-theme macrostructure (shown in bold). In the original development and presentation to largely information and communication professional groups the delivery sequence was slightly modified from that presented in the present summary.

The module structure

As a pedagogical tool and framework for learning in higher education three criteria need to be addressed: the delivery of appropriate content in terms of 'information-professional subject material' and domain content; the alignment of empirical material to suitable frameworks of reference (meaningful theoretical and practitioner frameworks); and the possibility of assimilation of both of these prior aspects to a cognitive framework for

PART 1: INFORMATION AND KNOWLEDGE MANAGEMENT
Unit 1 Information and Knowledge Management

PART 2: RESOURCES, PRODUCERS AND USERS
Unit 2 Information resources: producers and users
Unit 3 Information and communication skills

PART 3: TECHNOLOGY AND THE DIGITAL INFORMATION ECONOMY
Unit 4 ICTs and the digital environment

PART 4: ORGANIZING INFORMATION IN PRACTICE
Unit 5 Intelligence gathering and knowledge development
Unit 6 Organizing information in practice

PART 5: INFORMATION SERVICES
Unit 7 Dissemination, projection and mediation
Unit 8 Writing, editing and publishing
Unit 9 Networking and consultancy

PART 6: STRATEGY, POLICY AND PLANNING
Unit 10 Strategy, policy and planning
Unit 11 Media and press relations and practice
Unit 12 Resourcing information and communication activities
Unit 13 Performance measurement
Unit 14 Evaluation of corporate information activities.

Figure 9.1 *The 14-theme PIIK model*

practical articulation. This latter criterion would become the basis for the 'mapping' requirement: in another view, how to replace and/or advance the traditional mapping model with one suitable for the digital age.

If IL is to be embedded in the education and learning process it has to be shaped around the relationship between content and information process with clear goals, tasks and experiences, assessment and finally a delivery around learning outcomes. This illustration can be generalized to any profession or occupation (*domain*).

The *aims* of the PIIK module were:

- to provide students with an introduction to the concepts of information, intelligence and knowledge management by outlining contexts, development and fundamental principles
- to explore the methods, techniques and circumstances in which information, intelligence and knowledge management principles can be applied to the *domain*
- to provide a range of views on the social, behavioural and organizational conditions associated with information and knowledge management in the *domain*

- to critically analyse the way in which companies, other organizations (for example non-governmental organizations or NGOs) and individuals select and promote data, and to examine the dilemmas which ensue
- to explore the capacity of ICTs and information-handling tools and techniques to support knowledge management and to meet the knowledge needs of client communities, *domains of practice* and individuals
- to identify and develop criteria on which the basis of information, intelligence and knowledge-management activities can be evaluated
- to evaluate the impact of information, intelligence and knowledge management strategies, resources and techniques on client communities, individuals and *domains of practice*.

The *learning outcomes* of the PIIK module were specified to achieve the following outcomes:

- distinguish the distinctive characteristics of information, intelligence and knowledge management and locate them in the context of the *domain* (LO1)
- give an account of the domain of knowledge management as a synthesis of information management, social and organizational activities, and the achievement of specified goals (LO2)
- identify and evaluate representative sources within the information, intelligence and knowledge resource (LO3)
- be able to identify and elicit intelligence needs, and research and collect relevant knowledge from a range of primary and secondary sources (LO4)
- be able to evaluate sources of data and information to ensure reliability and validity of materials, detecting and alerting clients to discrepancies in the data (LO5)
- understand representative methods of information, intelligence and knowledge capture and to contextualize these as knowledge-seeking strategies applicable to the needs of the *domain* (LO6)
- offer an information/knowledge management strategy as appropriate to a given context and/or client and/or problem (LO7)
- demonstrate a practical understanding of the behaviour required of *domain* knowledge workers in representative contexts (LO8)
- present a coherent account of an information and knowledge management scenario in a given *domain of practice* and/or client community (LO9)
- be able to make critical and evaluative statements to support and justify the strategy proposed and the solutions adopted (LO10)

- be able to prepare and present reports to their clients (LO11).

Although it was designed for a specific course and group, a reflection on the aims and outcomes from the module suggest robust generic elements that can be transferred to other contexts of application. These provide a common conceptual foundation for information and communication tasks and when understood and practised should enhance the graduate's and professional's capacity to engage actively and interactively with content and process. Think of it as enhancing the cognitive tool set, encouraging engagement with both mapping personal spatial awareness of information and gaining experience of the links between professional task, information requirements, fulfilment of needs and realizing the benefits of information and communication behaviour in task performance. The following section suggests how content and process can be exploited and used in any domain.

Content and process in PIIK

The sequence shown here forms a 'meta-model' upon which more specific and detailed IL training and tasks are implemented and executed as the means to develop competences which can then be practised in the professional domain. In this example, the definitions in Part 1 are presented in more detail as defining the foundation. Each subsequent part would be expanded as necessary in any specific IL initiative and/or setting.

Part 1: Information and knowledge management

The terms 'Information and knowledge management', used so profusely by information professionals, is likely to be opaque and mysterious to the user (the citizen, the client, the customer, the professional). So the first task is to explain and demystify the term. What are the essential concepts and components? Content is normally the default basis of user satisfaction. 'I want to know about' is normally followed by a statement suggesting that content (informing material) is the representation of 'about-ness'. If 'stuff' is too demotic a word we at least know what its properties are. If useful it forms a basis: if not it can be rejected or reserved. Informed professional behaviour expects the manifestation of such competence in using 'information' in any task context.

A working definition can be provided by the following:

Data: Units of information in their simplest forms such as single observations, measurements, numerical identities, records of events. In order to fully comprehend their meaning or to access compound meanings aggregation and supplementation with other data, information and intelligence may be required.

Information: Aggregations of data in numerical, linguistic or symbolic form which have a meaningful capacity and which inform the receiver or user in a substantial way about things and matters in a specific way. Information may exist in more or less structured ways and may or may not be formally published, distributed or disseminated.

Intelligence: Data, information and sometimes knowledge which may be actually or potentially useful, but often requiring supplementation, confirmation and inference before its meaning can be fully ascertained or assured.

Knowledge: Things which are known as a result of experience and action and which are normally derived from sensory and intellectual input, which may be revealed through evidence in the form of data, information and intelligence. Knowledge often requires a temporal period for its construction, confirmation and affirmation. Knowledge can be enhanced through reflection, review and critical analysis as well as through exchange, sharing and collaboration. In the longer term knowledge is formed by constructive social engagement and socially constructed engagement.

The ability to identify, reflect and engage with these concepts has fundamental importance in any or many professional identities (of course any user has multiple identities: this is a certainty).

These forms of content provide the components for understanding as they lead on to further questions and identities which are embedded in subsequent transactional process. This process is one of antecedents, resolutions and consequences, which can relate both to material content as well as to communications and behaviours. These form the basis which leads towards and integrates in an *information and communication cycle* (ICC).

The information and communication cycle (the ICC model) is a generic model encompassing processes of information production, distribution, collection, storage, retrieval, dissemination and utilization. Utilization and action generates the next rotation of the cycle. Informational content passes through the phases of the model mediated by acts of communication and its management (handling) is represented by structures within and between stages of the process. There are many ways to illustrate such a cycle visually. The combination of content and cycle (in the ICC) is held in play by two fundamental processes of regulation which provide the means to stability and equilibrium and of dynamic adjustment. These processes are information management (and its varieties) and knowledge management (and its parallel varieties).

Information management: This term has come to mean the systematic approach to the identification, acquisition, processing, storage, analysis, retrieval, distribution and dissemination of data, information and intelligence (and to some extent knowledge) in order to exploit information as a resource, making it resourceful for strategic purposes, extracting value and attaining impact. The management of information implies a necessary engagement with and management of the media in which the information is contained. This provides a basis for incorporating librarianship and documentation within the sphere of information management. In order to obtain the maximum benefits information management tasks have become professionalized to make the best use of technologies, systems, methods and techniques.

Knowledge management: This represents a progressively more coherent, strategic and purposive effort to extend the base of information management (and its business equivalent in Information Resource Management (IRM) to encompass knowledge in all its forms, aspects and varieties. The totality of knowledge resources may be referred to as intellectual capital and are combined with human, structural and customer capital resources to obtain the maximum benefits from all human knowledge. Its foci include the management of existing knowledge resources through sharing, leveraging, collaborating and learning in order to create new knowledge to provide a basis for innovation and progress and increases in economic, social and cultural welfare.

The relevance of the ICC model to information management (IM) lies in the relations between the information itself and preceding and subsequent stages of any element of the model. At each stage processing takes place, with the potential to optimize the outcomes achievable through acts of information management. A similar relationship to knowledge management (KM) can be discerned, although influenced by many more intangible, subjective and extraneous factors.

The constituents of models of information and communication enable any given information management (and knowledge management) activity to be isolated and placed in its overall context. The ability to identify and describe the greater system (macro system) and to locate individual elements within the system provides a valuable diagnostic tool to consider operational problems within information management and its *organizational setting*. In terms of developing IP competences as a part of a professional's resources, the framework will provide structures that each professional can assimilate and apply. Embedding these structures opens the way to exploring and mapping information and knowledge spaces. It provides a vocabulary for development.

What follows is an illustrative rationale for the rest of the module scheme (of course, capable of much more extended development!).

Part 2: Resources, producers and users

Unit 2 (Information resources: producers and users) addresses the fundamental cyclical relationship. Information production comes from user activity and reflection on user behaviour and process is the key to comprehending production. Unit 3 (Information and communication skills) can develop a more conscious awareness of 'being a user' and understanding the nature and power of information and communication behaviours. An understanding of resources can be gained through audit methods and this part comprehends all kinds of libraries, service providers and information sources.

Part 3: Technology and the digital information economy

Unit 4 (ICTs and the digital environment) impresses the idea of technology literacy and behaviour and can show the link between the individual and the collective (linking informal and social behaviours to formal and collective information acts). Given the rapid absorption of 'digital' within professional environments this aspect has relevance which generates motivation to learn and progress.

Part 4: Organizing information in practice

Unit 5 (Intelligence gathering and knowledge development) provides scope for an appreciation of the way tasks and work are intimately related to information and how the interaction and management of external resources is enhanced by a more conscious engagement with information. The 'citizenships of information' are intimately related to the organization and management tasks in practice (Unit 6: Organizing information in practice).

Part 5: Information services

Writing, editing and publishing (Unit 8) explores the role of the individual professional as producer and consciousness of this phase produces interaction with sources and resources at the collective scale and links the individual to service and dissemination (Unit 7: Dissemination, projection and mediation). Entering into the dynamic of creation and production provides the motivation for professionals to network (Unit 9: Networking and consultancy). At the individual and personal level a 'one-on-one' dialogue is 'information service' (requiring communication and interpersonal skills). At the collective level a library as much as digital source is providing information service. The well understood distinction between 'formal' and informal' communication is thus eternally present. We read and value 'formal' text as much as we can and do value oral communication, broadcast communication and even gossip on the grapevine. These are all aspects of the professional domain as much as the personal one! If it is done well and it is valued we consider it competent: if it is less so, then it demands an improvement in literacy.

This historical idea of 'information service' as collective provision for individual use is evolving towards the view that each individual becomes a basis to provide service in the form of transactions of information both to other individuals and to the collective. Both elements will exist and can be drawn upon. Historically the IL task has been significantly derived from mastery of technique. Now and in the future the shaping and changes to be made will address behaviours and thereby motivate the use and exploitation of technique.

Part 6: Strategy, policy and planning

The sixth part illuminates a number of holistic dimensions which are manifest in wider propagation of communication and information (for example, Unit 11: Media and press relations and practice), and the need to engage in collective activities of information provision and management, including IM and KM at various levels (for example, Unit 12: Resourcing information and communication activities). With an enhanced awareness of information and communication and the realization of desirable (learned) outcomes an interest in performance measurement (Unit 13) and evaluation of individual and corporate information activities (Unit 14) provides a natural conclusion to endeavours. The PIIK test group of students of corporate communication encouraged a very close fit between technique, motivation and behaviour. Advocating PIIK as a model for other domains will call for adaptation to the user and professional circumstances encountered. The traditional advocates of IL faced the same challenge but we might see the future as more hopeful of success if relevance, motivation and behavioural change are more strongly weighted.

In order to demonstrate learning outcomes the PIIK module required students to submit two assessments, including an oral presentation.

- **Element One** (Information and intelligence report) was designed to develop a primary understanding of the nature, provenance and quality of information relevant to the issues on hand. It provided an opportunity to use the initial range of themes and content covered in the module as tools to assist the development of information- and knowledge-management aspects of corporate communication in general and in the assignment setting.
- **Element Two** (Information and knowledge management strategy and policy) enabled the learner to build upon the first assignment by identifying a strategic context within the domain elements (corporate communication in the tested case), and then passing to the main aim of the assignment: to develop and critically analyse an information- and knowledge-management strategy and policy which is relevant to the chosen corporate communication challenge.

These assignments provide a generic template for developing IP competences in domain professionals. Element One provides the essentials of framework, technique and content. Element Two is premised on a developing sense of ownership and responsibility which through a strategic focus develops motivation, professional response and effective behaviour. The student as impending professional selects the case and thus the content and the context. The result must be a solution to the problem, but must also be open to those identified means which improve professional practice. In the PIIK test case the assignment specifications produced the expected outcomes. The module earned credits (20) which contributed to the 180 required for a Master's degree. Of course PIIK was a one-off initiative but it ran for 12 years, was valid for Chartered Institute of Public Relations (CIPR) accreditation and was externally examined and reviewed over the years by an industry panel. As is often the case, market demands change and recruitment targets halted the progress of the Master's course and the module. To be sure, the module could hardly have thrived without being taught by 'professional library and information educators' but surely this is a point to validate the contribution of IP expertise in general higher education?

The models of content provide linear stability and the models of management provide a dynamic structure to engage in the uncertainty of real-life behaviour. Most fortunately, the techniques of information audit provide a means to empirically explore and verify the components of any given domain of information, knowledge and communication behaviour. This offers a flexible metric to engage with information and to apply it to needs by exploiting the value which is embedded and added. Familiarity and practice will enable the user and learner with a means to map the information and communication terrain and engage with any given level. If designers can develop their tools within the structure there is a greater likelihood that those who possess information and knowledge resources can establish a mutual meeting point.

Information Literacy and workplace development

Such a proposal, when offered to relevant higher education institutions and to individual educators and information professionals, has the considerable advantage of a practical, empirical foundation, albeit only one. It stands as one of many initiatives in user education and IL which is now a massive body and community of practice. The potential value is that it was 'lived and studied' as a 20-credit taught module at Level 7 and was delivered in a validated professional course (CIPR) and was externally examined. It was realized that this route is necessarily labour intensive and that it exposed the tension between more proactive students and those who focused on studying little more than the desired or normative professional curriculum, and indeed who were understandably resistant to 'mind-bending' by an information professional educator. But there were enough signs that for students who would make the effort to bend there were rewards and satisfactions.

What might the experience of teaching the PIIK module in the 2000s suggest to IL practitioners as we close in on the third decade of the century? The 'user' (lived) experience of information has undergone a structural shift – a generational shift – over 20 years. In 2000 the internet and ICT were still innovative and novel. By 2016 we are ever closer to a digitally normative society, at least in the global North, but the global South is catching up. There is an abundance of commentators and critics in every media forum and continuing technology innovation. It may not quite be a binary choice of 'it's the digital economy now' or 'don't look backwards to the past'! We cannot irrevocably say that 'digital satisfies' and that artificial intelligence will become superior to human intelligence, but we are at a hinge point.

The contemporary practice of IL needs to identify the best of the past and see how it can play a part in the future. We have more information, but do we have more wisdom? The user 'now' is more empowered than the user 'then', whenever that was, but psychologically little has changed. New times will need new cognitive and information spatial mappings, but they are likely to remain rooted in some eternal concepts and constructs. There will still be the 'information and communication cycle' and this is likely to be a place for the PIIK agenda to play its part in information.

As a reflection on a past IL pedagogy and an appraisal of the context faced in contemporary higher education, what conclusion can be drawn and what markers can be laid down?

- In an era of higher education which makes substantial claims for its vital role in employability and the development of modern professionals in any domain, the experience of a 'PIIK-type' approach is relevant. IP knowledge needs to be presented and refined in substance and vocabulary not only to assure its propagation but also to offer some sense that sufficient deeper cognitive knowledge is not remote from a field of practice. If not the 'PIIK- type', then what can improve it and if necessary substitute it as a model?
- The operational model is one of 'informed information citizenship'. This can only be achieved by admitting the significance, depth and possible challenge of the task. If the IP and IL world can make the case (which it clearly believes it can) then there is a responsibility to continue to promote its case. A practical way to do this is for IP and IL specialists to raise their profile in engaging with audiences in the professions, in tertiary education and in public fora.
- In a setting where not only is 'digital' the norm and one in which the immediate current and growing speculation is about the scope and inevitability for artificial intelligence (AI) to play a more substantial part, we must neither not lose sight of the individual and the person (human and citizen) nor eject the place and part of traditional and physical information cultures from their legitimate role. We have become all too accustomed to the refrain that 'information is the future', to the extent that to replace it by the slogan 'knowledge is the future' is perhaps to add very little. What will be the constant is the 'human and citizen' and thus the aspiration for all to be generally informed and literate is enduringly valid.
- Making sure that those fortunate to receive higher education and to aspire to be 'professional' are given the best chances in their formative years and are able to acquire competence and knowledge of the kind envisaged in the opportunity the 'PIIK-type' gave to a particular cohort in higher education. This serves to link the IL experiences of the primary and secondary periods of education with the worlds of work and employment generally and with those of the 'professionally skilled'.

CHAPTER 10

The 'hidden' value of Information Literacy in the workplace context: how to unlock and create value

Bonnie Cheuk

This chapter will discuss:

- how there are many knowledge workers in the business world who are not traditionally considered information professionals but use information as part of their day-to-day work.
- how information professionals might play a business-driven, strategic yet pragmatic role in the enhancement of the Information Literacy (IL) capabilities of knowledge workers of all types and levels.

Introduction

The job titles of information professionals are numerous and varied: from strategist, information/knowledge manager, intranet/internet manager, professional support lawyer, to CRM administrator, researcher, analyst, marketing and communication manager, product manager, training manager and many more. In this chapter, information professionals are defined as those key employees of whatever label who consciously consider how best to help the company leverage information and/or create information systems, service and marketplace to create value for their employees, clients or business stakeholders. There are many knowledge workers who are not traditionally considered information professionals but use information as part of their day-to-day work.

As the advancement of technology empowers all knowledge workers with affordable digital tools at their fingertips, information professionals are increasingly providing coaching and training services on the effective use of information systems (where the information is stored) or communication tools (where ideas and information are exchanged). They offer advice on how to create, share, search, organize, visualize, analyse and present information. Simply speaking, they show themselves to be those pivotal individuals who introduce 'Information Literacy' to the workplace context.

So how important is IL in the workplace context? This chapter examines knowledge workers in different roles, functions and levels, who work under different operating models and company cultures, to understand if and when IL adds value to the business, and if it does, how might information professionals play a business-driven, strategic yet pragmatic role to enhance knowledge workers' IL capabilities.

If IL is important in the digital world, why is it so hidden? Why don't we see 'Information Literacy' in the training catalogue? Why don't we see the phrase appearing in job descriptions, or listed as an essential skill similar to 'communication skills', 'time management', 'project management', 'ability to use MS Access or Excel'? It remains clear that IL is hidden within the business context; it is so embedded in the business activities that one cannot talk about it meaningfully as a separate phenomenon.

This chapter proposes that IL models borrowed from the academic context are unlikely to meet the changing definition of information and the dynamics of information need experienced by knowledge workers in the wide variety of contemporary contexts. A refined definition of IL in the workplace is put forward, followed by a practical case study to illustrate how a multinational corporation might successfully roll out an IL programme in the form of, one might even say 'disguised as', a 'change management' intervention in the context of an attempt at broader business culture change.

The chapter ends with a set of recommendations for IL experts, researchers, academics and industry practitioners which will assist in the development of information-literate, effectively information-driven organizations.

Let's be honest: we have a problem

Let's be honest: **we have a problem with Information Literacy in the workplace context**. My career as an information professional has ranged widely, covering government, non-profit and business organizations around the globe in the past 20 years. After a PhD in information science, I moved into a large US global consulting firm, supporting the partners, and then managing, and eventually directing knowledge management programmes for multinational companies. Later in my career I had the opportunity to work as an 'intrapreneur' within global companies (in the consulting industry, financial services and the government sector), taking up a senior management role focusing on driving business transformation through creating value from information, enabled by digital technologies.

My personal journey, my interaction with other information professionals working in the business setting, and my research into recent development on IL in the workplace context, has lead me to the following conclusions:

1   There is a problem with IL in the workplace context. IL experts speak only to ourselves, and mostly in an academic context. We have not done enough to help the business world to understand what IL is, and what value it can add.
2   The phrase 'Information Literacy' does not mean anything in the business context. Business CEOs do not know what it means, so they will not pay attention to it.

I do not think we should despair; the language should not get in the way. There are several potential solutions:

1   To make it worthwhile investing in IL, we need to show it can add real value for businesses and their employees, clients and stakeholders.
2   Even if the value of 'Information Literacy' is clear, we need to be mindful that it is disguised under many different labels. We need to refer to IL in business language which a corporation's most important senior executives (often referred to as the 'C-Suite'), managers, executives and knowledge workers can understand. This could mean not using the phrase 'Information Literacy' at all.
3   We should recognize that how information is defined and labelled differs in different business scenarios.
4   Information professionals should be brave and admit that we have made limited progress (when compared to academic settings) in putting IL on the strategic agenda and getting the attention of the C-Suite. We must rethink our current practices to avoid getting stuck in the current unacceptable situation for another 10–20 years.
5   As the digital revolution puts information tools and sources at everyone's fingertips, we have an opportunity to up the game and demonstrate the value of information and promote IL in the modern, networked workplace.
6   Information professionals have the opportunity to become trusted strategic advisers and coaches, who can empower senior executives and knowledge workers at all levels to create value from the world of abundant information, enabled by emerging technologies.
7   This journey is not going to be easy. It requires vision, leadership, business and political acumen and excellent communication and change management skills. Information professionals have to get 'under the skin' of each business and be business-focused. They must understand the nature of information, IL research, theories and practices, and be

able to translate this into the workplace context. Where gaps remain, new theories and practices have to be developed. It is an exciting time for the profession!

Some good news

Some good news: Information Literacy is a key workplace attribute, it just doesn't have that label. According to the American Library Association, IL is a set of abilities requiring individuals to 'recognize when information is needed and have the ability to locate, evaluate, and use effectively the needed information' (ACRL, 2000). How important is this set of abilities in the business setting? Let us look at some recent trends:

- According to IBM, in 2016 we created 2.5 quintillion bytes of data each day. Of the data in the world today, 90% has been created in the last two years alone.
- In June 2016, the European Commission set out steps to improve digital skills in Europe, which are the cornerstone of a truly functioning digital society. The aim is to upgrade skills in using information and communication technologies (ICT) (European Commission, 2016).

With the rise of mobile devices and Web 2.0 technologies, individuals have online information at their fingertips. What could their experience with information be like? Perhaps they are confident information users with skills to use digital tools effectively, and take control of information available to achieve their goals. Or are they overwhelmed by the sheer amount of information, stressed out by new technologies, and so unable to put information available into good use?

The need for knowledge workers to have 'digital skills' and 'ICT literacy' to access and use information is widely recognized in the workplace. Whilst the phrase 'Information Literacy' is not commonly used, the focus on improving digital skills implies the need to frequently use digital tools to interact with information to get their work done. Information Literacy is more important than ever before.

Information Literacy inside the organization

How is IL inside the organization different from that in academic settings? In the academic setting, effective use of information is about searching, analysing, summarizing, consolidating and presenting information for learning and research purposes. Information tends to be stored in books, library and information systems, personal online and mobile devices, communication channels and social networks. The student learns to go through these iterative steps as an individual or in a group setting. By going through these interactive stages during the research process, the student acquires new knowledge and develops lifelong learning skills.

In a workplace setting, the primary goal of knowledge workers is not focused on learning in the academic sense of personal development. It is about getting business done; achieving goals and targets with resources available. The need to access, interact, use and present information, enabled by a range of business applications and ICT technologies, is a means to an end. From strategic planning, innovation, sales, product development and customer service to business operations, knowledge workers have to interact with information, sometimes as individuals, other times as a team, to get their work done.

The challenge of introducing IL in the workplace comes from the dynamic nature of information. How is information defined? What information is needed? How should it be put to use? Different business settings give different responses. A one-size-fit-all IL definition borrowed from the academic context does not apply.

What factors impact on how knowledge workers experience information every day? They can be summarized as:

- role and business functions
- the business operating model
- the company culture.

Information Literacy in the workplace is disguised

Information Literacy in the workplace is disguised within different business activities, roles and functions. At the highest level within the organization, senior executives have to use information to inform strategic decisions every day. They assemble teams to conduct market analysis, competitor-watch and brand monitoring. The information is organized and visualized in an impactful way, and shared with the board or key stakeholders, to help to spot opportunities and threats, to inform decisions or to adjust strategic plans.

In the areas of innovation, research and development, sales and marketing and product management, marketers, researchers, product managers, consultants and analysts are constantly watching trends in the marketplace and assess their impact on current services/products and opportunities to create additional value for employees, customers and stakeholders. They conduct primary and secondary research, customer surveys, monitor clients, set up alerts, access internal and external information sources, subscribe to research services, attend conferences, etc. Very often, the information they receive is incomplete; they have to draw on their experience to make judgement calls.

In the area of learning and development which aims to increase staff capabilities, trainers and learners have to interact with information and exchange ideas with one another. Trainers typically need to understand business goals, analyse skills gaps, and do other research to develop training materials. Learners need to organize their own learning, search for training materials, reflect and practise newly acquired skills.

On an operational level, frontline staff, operators and customer service representatives need to understand customers' needs and know what services and products can be offered to meet their needs. They need to observe and gain insights into changing customers' needs and behaviours, and provide feedback to management to drive continuous improvement, or to put forward ideas to address customer complaints or innovate new approaches to transform customer services.

Regardless of their function, knowledge workers have to interact with information all the time. However, these information activities are disguised under different labels, e.g. market research, data analytics, environment scanning, strategic planning, customer service, innovation, communication, training, analytics, etc. One has to see through these labels to see the nature of the IL required in the workplace; one must:

- recognize the need for information: when to look for answers, when to call in experts, when to do more research, and when to stop looking for information and make a decision based on incomplete information
- conduct research to fill the gaps via multiple channels, including accessing subject matter experts and external consultants
- look for information stored in information or communication systems or in other people's heads. This includes using a range of business applications and ICT tools provided by the company (or increasingly via personal mobile devices) to access information, to engage in conversation online and to discuss face-to-face
- assess the quality and reliability of the information, be able to separate comments from facts and recognize that the criteria change in different contexts
- present the information in an impactful way to help others make sense of it, to see patterns, gain insights and ultimately to inform decision making or call for actions
- organize information to enhance one's learning, to facilitate information re-use or for future reference by oneself or other colleagues
- engage with information at different times on a personal level, team or company-wide level.

Different models for different contexts

What is information? Information is anything that can help knowledge workers make sense of their working life (Cheuk and Dervin, 2011). Information can be facts, comments, data, content, insights, answers, hunches or a supporting message. Information Literacy requires knowledge workers' ability to interact with all of these types of information under different operating models.

Four operating zones are presented below (Cheuk, 2016), informed by Snowden's Cynefin framework (Snowden and Boone, 2007) and Moore's innovation framework (Moore, 2015). These four zones can be found in all companies. Each zone outlines the different type of information required for knowledge workers to make sense of their world, and therefore the experiences of IL:

1   **In the efficiency zone**, the company knows exactly what needs to be done, and how to achieve the goal with the lowest cost and resources. Typically, companies put in place procedures to achieve precise, desirable outcomes. Typical business activities that come under this zone include the product helpdesk, systems administration, manufacturing production line management, and executing finance, procurement, legal or payment processes. In this zone, companies want their employees to use the right information and to follow established steps to achieve well defined positive business outcomes. When talking about looking for information in this zone, the expectation is about knowing exactly where, and from whom, one can find the right answers and procedures. The expectation is zero deviance from the procedures.
2   **In the effectiveness zone**, the company knows exactly what needs to be done, and knows that by adopting a new practice, the outcomes will certainly improve. Typical business activities include adopting a new part in a machine to improve its lifespan, introducing a new channel for customers to place orders and rolling out a new CRM system to capture sales activities. In this zone, knowledge workers need to find out what works, and then apply it, taking into consideration the geographical, functional and cultural context. The ability to quickly transfer the new practice from one context to another creates most value. Information work in this zone is about accessing best practices or recipes for success.
3   **In the innovation zone**, the company is entering a new territory and trying out new ideas or practices. There is no right answer, it is an experimental journey. Typical examples are business transformation activities such as entering a new market, introducing a new organization design or developing a new product to see if it may gain traction with target customers. In this zone, knowledge workers have to

look inside, outside and at unexpected places to find new ideas. They could be reading external research reports, attending conferences to discover what other companies are doing, following thought leaders' blogs and social media sites, or setting up confidential reference visits/meetings with potential customers, partners or investors. In this zone, the focus is on digesting diverse ideas, experimenting, and sensing the signal and making adjustments quickly. The 'answer' does not yet exist, the destination is not defined, future knowledge has yet to be created.

4   **In the chaotic zone**, situations do not make immediate sense and one does not know how to handle them, as they have never happened before. A typical example is when a company finds itself in a crisis situation due to something dramatic and unexpected having happened. To prevent the situation deteriorating, immediate action is required; any extended analysis must come later. This zone is about taking decisive action now – there is no time to research – drawing on best judgement and incomplete information. Very often, as the crisis unfolds one has to ignore the information available, as it does not appear to make sense.

These four zones outline the dimensions of IL in the business workplace. Significantly, the definition of information differs in each zone:

1   In the efficiency zone, information is the correct procedure one must follow. Seeking and using information is a straightforward search-and-find-the-answer process.
2   In the effectiveness zone, information is best practice, which one can learn and replicate to improve or to solve a problem. Information seeking and using is about conducting research and networking with the experienced practitioners, and then applying the information in the new context.
3   In the innovation zone, information is defined as 'potential ideas' or 'possibilities'. The certainty level and reliability of the information cannot be assessed. There are no right answers or good practices to search for, but only experimenting and creating new knowledge and practices.
4   In the chaotic zone, information does not even make sense. One has to abandon looking for information and take decisive actions right away.

Interestingly, zones 1 to 3, in general terms but also in their increasing complexity of IL experience, can be seen to parallel Forster's nursing study (Forster, 2015a): this despite the radically different purposes and aims in healthcare and business workplaces.

The changing definition of information in the four different zones reminds us of the difficulty in applying a one-size-fits-all model to IL in the workplace. The embeddedness of information in the business context makes it impossible to talk about 'information' or 'Information Literacy' out of context.

Information Literacy requirements in different company cultures

In the academic setting, IL is regarded as a positive attribute. Students are expected to acquire or demonstrate IL in their learning process. Does this same principle apply in the workplace? If knowledge workers are not information-literate, is this a problem on its own or is it a symptom of a bigger problem?

Applying Dervin's Sense-Making Methodology (Dervin, 2003), knowledge workers can make sense of their world. When they see a gap, they will reach out to the channels, sources and help they need. If one does not identify a need for information, or interact with information, this may be for a number of reasons:

- The knowledge worker does not see any deficit, and therefore there is no need to seek information; he or she may be working on a very stable, predictable environment.
- The knowledge worker does see a deficit; however, she or he does not feel anything can be done to address it. This could be because the person is not empowered to propose ideas or to take actions to rectify the problem. This typically happens in the productivity zone, when knowledge workers are expected only to follow procedures.
- The knowledge worker does not get the information and help from experts that is needed, as the information and expertise do not exist.
- The knowledge worker does not get the information he or she needs, because information and communication systems and experts are impossible to use effectively.
- Knowledge workers cannot make sense of information in a 'chaotic zone' crisis situation.

Company culture influences knowledge workers' behaviours. Some companies value information: the senior executives promote the flow of information and ideas across organization divisional boundaries, promote discussion and debate, and invest in information technologies and services to enable information flow, including encouraging people-to-peer connections. They believe the flow of information across boundaries allows the company to be more agile and responsive to disruptive changes. IL is a foundational requirement in this culture; it is being cherished. Other companies, although claiming that they are information-driven, may see information purely as an asset reserved for senior managers. They will adopt a command-and-control management model which leaves limited or no decision-making power to the lower-ranking staff. Such a culture tends to be supported by hierarchically controlled information and communication systems, whereby information is controlled and visible to the senior management team or their delegates only. In this culture, IL is not a requirement for all knowledge workers, as the need to seek for information to address any issues is tightly managed.

Whilst knowledge workers may widely engage with information in their personal lives, once they step into the office their choices are constrained by the company culture; the information ecology provided by the company, as well as legal and compliance requirements related to their industry. This has huge implications in how to promote IL in the workplace.

Redefining Information Literacy in the workplace context

Through understanding the factors that influence the definition of information and how information is being used, the following definition of IL at work is proposed. This definition is informed by a thorough review of IL in the workplace and influenced by Dervin's user-centric Sense-making Methodology (Cheuk and Dervin, 2011):

- Information Literacy is not a goal on its own in the workplace context, it is a means to get work done in specific business contexts. Information is created and used to make decisions or influence others in their decision-making process. This use of information is enabled by digital technologies, and therefore digital skills are essential. Effective two-way communication skills are also critical.
- In the process of getting work done, knowledge workers encounter gaps, questions, worries and struggles. They need to find ways to fill the gaps by reaching through a range of channels and sources (internal and external, human and technological), and assess and evaluate the knowledge, comments, facts, empathy, feelings, answers and support they obtain.
- Ultimately, knowledge workers need to draw conclusions, take action and make decisions based on the information obtained. In some cases, they have to ignore the information in order to stop a crisis situation.
- The ability to make business ideas accessible (i.e. 'to get the message across') and to influence other teams to take action is critical. The knowledge worker has to synthesize and present information effectively to other business stakeholders, peers or senior managers.

- When the required skills are not available, external experts are in-sourced.
- Ultimately, whether Information Literacy is required in the workplace context is influenced by the company culture and technologies provided, as well as legal and regulatory requirements.

The phrase 'Information Literacy' does not mean anything to knowledge workers; IL attributes are disguised within different labels and business processes which are specific to the business context.

Introducing a meaningful concept of Information Literacy

How can we introduce a concept of IL that is meaningful to the C-Suite and knowledge workers? It is clear that an IL promotional endeavour will only gain attention if it is seen as contributing to getting work done in a business context. How can this be achieved?

The following critical success factors must be addressed:

1 All business activities require knowledge workers to interact and use different types of information, and therefore IL is a must. However, there is no point referring to 'Information Literacy' as a separate label. The focus should be placed on *how best to use information to deliver the highest priority strategic goals for the company* to achieve positive business impact, rather than trying to do too much in a generic way. Information professionals must keep asking and pushing the question: 'How we can make the best use of information to achieve [business goals *x*]'. For example: How can we better understand clients' needs? How can we commercialize the information we have? How can we gain better insight and share them to call for action?

2 Once the strategic information management policy is clearly defined by the company, information professionals might consider introducing IL under the name of 'change management'. Whether the business case focuses on improving employee engagement, increasing sales revenue, faster response times to customers' problems, faster product innovation or improving operational efficiency, such priorities will provide a focus on how best to use information to add value, transform business and/or change work practices. This can be translated into a range of interventions, such as information services and systems, training programmes or communication campaigns, to empower knowledge workers to create business value from the information available.

3 As new technologies continue to emerge, there is a sense of inadequacy amongst knowledge workers as they attempt to keep up with ever-

changing trends. Information Literacy can be positioned as a key aspect of 'digital skills' training, e.g. teaching knowledge workers how to use new information systems, new communication and collaboration tools and social networking platforms. The training does not need to be tools-focused. 'Digital tools' can be used as a hook to upgrade knowledge workers' IL skills. As these tools are introduced, the rationale and benefits of sharing information and creating value are highlighted. The training places the greatest emphasis on 'why', not 'how', one uses the tools. The training addresses why one should share or use the information which is made available by the particular tool, focusing on what business purpose is facilitated; that is, 'What is in it for me?', and 'How would it add business value and increase my personal/team productivity and effectiveness?', and 'How can I improve my personal information environment?'. This is a departure from the traditional training practice in academic settings (e.g. how to use the online library catalogue, how to use specialized databases).

4   Position IL as a 'big data' initiative which gives 360-degree perspectives of customers' needs. This brings out knowledge workers' awareness of the information residing in a range of fragmented sources and locations, which when strategically bundled together can offer insight to inform strategic planning. This means information professionals have to partner with other experts in business intelligence and analytics to turn information seeking and critique into actionable insights.

5   Position IL as a taking control of the information environment, allowing the organization to avoid information overload problems. Learning to take control means moving from a 'push' to a 'pull' environment, whereby knowledge workers move away from being passive recipients of information and actively decide what activities one should monitor to ensure the relevant information appears on one's radar. This can mean conducting one-on-one coaching with C-level executives to help them to reflect on their strategic goals, their needs, and how information flows to them, the tools they use, how best to set up streams and subscriptions to have a real-time dashboard to discover relevant information both from within and outside the company.

6   As information forms the fabric of management practice, IL needs to be embedded into leadership development programmes. To function effectively as a leader in a world of information abundance, leaders need to learn to listen to diverse viewpoints, to be able to promote dialogue between knowledge workers with different views and to be humble enough to ensure that the power they hold does not silence minority voices and unwelcome viewpoints. Leaders also need to undo processes of hoarding information and share the 'information power',

while remaining conscious of the risks inherent in sharing information. A conscious attempt to embed this mindset and these communication practices within leaders' behaviour introduces IL in a subtle way.

In the next section, a case study is used to illustrate how IL can be introduced to a global company in this 'disguised' way, as part of a broader cultural change program.

Case study: an Information Literacy development programme in the workplace

Global financial companies have a strategic need to become increasingly agile, collaborative and engaged, in response to changing external environments, clients' needs and regulatory requirements. The company in which this case study is located was in the process of rolling out a series of cultural change programmes to future-proof their business.

Supported by the CEO, Chief Operating Officer and Chief HR Officer, a new social intranet and collaboration platform (named 'Pulse+') was positioned as a platform for change, liberating communication, top-down and bottom-up. It is a knowledge-sharing and collaboration ecosystem that empowers employees and puts them in control – colleagues can connect, communicate and collaborate effectively from anywhere, at any time. Pulse+ seamlessly links to productivity tools, so it's easy to get real work done.

From conception to roll-out, it took 12 months to set up the foundation for change. During this period, a global IL programme (branded as 'new ways of working change programme') was rolled out, to help employees understand why it is important to share and consume information at a personal and company level.

1   Through an understanding of this principle the Change Management Team recognized that the business context can be different for people in different functions and roles and different operating zones. The team created a dozen examples to illustrate when and why one must use the platform and how, in order to effectively share and find information and expert sources of information to create value. The examples included how to better use information to engage with all staff, how to better use information to innovate new products and services, how to interact and find information to improve people management skills, how to use information and interact to organize a conference, how to on-board new hires, and how to create a knowledge hub to share operational procedures.
2   Once knowledge workers understood the 'why', a digital skills training

programme was rolled out to explain the 'how to do it', using a range of new technologies. For example, 'How do I share a document?', 'How do I index?', 'How do I share?', 'How do I subscribe to information?', 'How do I use the mobile app?'. The digital skills training programme continued to reinforce the 'why' and the business-specific examples, and cover both desktop experience and mobile experience.

3   For senior executives, there was a one-hour one-on-one coaching session to identify their needs, their priorities, and how they could configure their information streams and subscription to achieve their goals. Having this discussion helped them to think about what internal and external information they needed, and the best way to access them. The goal was to help them to become autonomous, and not rely on information professionals or their assistants to get information for them. Follow-up meetings were set up on a quarterly basis to adjust their strategy.

4   In additional, a 'global champions network' was developed to share ideas and best practices in the introduction of IL in their division. They were the pioneers: trying out the experience themselves, leading by example and showing others they way.

5   The programme also highlighted the risk, compliance and regulatory requirements as to what kind of information could or could not be shared on Pulse+, and ensured that the knowledge workers understood the dos and don'ts.

6   As content and interaction occurred on Pulse+, the programme started to focus on sensing emerging patterns (e.g. tag clouds, hot topics, top liked content) and the change management team coached knowledge workers in how to monitor insights to discover what they did not know they didn't know. This is 'big data' in action.

7   In addition, the leaders of the company were invited to an experiential-learning leadership development programme to practise different ways to share ideas, have meaningful conversations and build on one another's ideas, and to be open to change and new ideas from other departments and outside the company. By embedding this thinking in their day-to-day work, they learned to be information-literate, especially in seeking ideas and sharing ideas both face-to-face and online.

8   It was not all smooth sailing. In the first year, there were many sceptical colleagues who questioned why one would bother sharing their information or ideas, or felt uncomfortable sharing work-in-progress. To address their needs, the Change Management Team showed them by means of one-to-one consultations how and why the sharing of information and information seeking was beneficial to them on a personal level, using real examples which made sense to their role and

function, and showing them examples from other leaders outside the company.

All in all, the IL programme looked very different from an IL programme in an academic setting. *It spoke in business language, took on a very business-driven, user-centric approach to help knowledge workers understand the benefits of interacting with information and people in a new way, helped them self-discover why they needed to change and stimulated their willingness to use information to deliver specific strategic goals.*

Lessons learned and implications for the future

What recommendations can be made to practitioners, researchers and policy makers who want to further develop IL programmes in the workplace context, and ultimately help their companies to build the capability to become an information-driven business?

1   Be an 'intrapreneur'; think at a senior executive level, as someone who understands the strategic goals of the company; and advocate running an information-driven business, promoting a culture of information flow in the workplace. Gain a seat at the table which has the influence and decision-making power, and continuously advocate the power of information to improve top-line and bottom-line company results.
2   Be conversant with the business language one operates in. Do not use any jargon, always translate IL principles into business language at all times.
3   Personally lead by example; demonstrate how the effective use and sharing of information can lead to positive outcomes. Be comfortable using new digital tools, and show empathy with other knowledge workers who may be struggling. Be a visible and empathetic coach, practise leadership through example to show others the way. Work with knowledge workers across all levels and cultures. Be seen as a leader who understands how to turn information into asset, and proactively help open the doors to ensure that the right tools, culture and ecology are put in place to support the business needs.
4   Be opportunistic, by leveraging the ever-changing technology landscape to continuously refresh knowledge workers' interest in IL. Where there is interest in learning about a new tool (e.g. social intranet, collaboration, messaging, analytics), or learning new ways to visualize information (e.g. infographics, word cloud, video, animation, virtual reality), always take the opportunity to discuss 'why' are we using these tools, to create what kind of value, and how one can be effective in interacting with information. The tools are only enablers.

5   Be a collaboration role model. Be a facilitator and politician who can bring different teams with different agendas together to create a common vision and align multiple information-related projects to create the ecology to allow information to flow across the company.
6   Be in touch with latest developments in IL and experts in the field, and translate the latest best practices into the workplace context. Go to business, practitioner and IL conferences to help bridge the gap and help companies to understand the value of using information to run a company.
7   For the senior executives who are promoting IL in the workplace, form a network to share practical experience and toolkits, case studies and methodologies.
8   Information Literacy experts in the academic context should consider increasing academic–industry research partnership. Create a cross-disciplinary think tank to bring business practitioners, academia and researchers together, with the aim to create a set of business-focused materials to promote IL at work, possibly starting with a specific function or role. Make IL practical for a specific function.
9   Information Literacy experts in the academic setting should revisit the existing IL curriculum and question if it provides enough business context and variation of business scenarios for students to practise IL in their future role. They should continue to embed IL in the curriculum, by discussing real-life scenarios, and reflecting on how one would search for and use information differently in different contexts and on what strategies work best in different situations. Such abilities can become habitual and then can be applied naturally at work.

Final words

For IL to be meaningful in the workplace, a company needs to embrace a culture which uses information to add value to the work and outcomes for employees, customers and stakeholders at all levels. Ultimately, information professionals need to find ways to influence and help C-Suite and board members to understand the benefits of creating value from information, using language that makes sense to them. Without this, information professionals' enthusiastic efforts to promote IL will not bear fruit, or the impact will be limited.

Whilst information professionals accept that IL in the workplace context is under-developed, if we address this by focusing only on IL definition, creating IL models, or teaching knowledge workers how to use digital tools, we may miss the bigger opportunity to start positioning IL as a company-wide strategy to create a knowledge-driven or information-driven organization.

The journey will be long and challenging. We can get there by making this happen one company at a time, one CEO at a time, and showcase examples in different business contexts that demonstrate positive outcomes. The opportunity is there for us to grab.

CHAPTER 11

The 'Workplace Experience Framework' and evidence-based Information Literacy education

Marc Forster

This chapter will discuss:

- a new approach to IL education for students and professionals based on detailed research into its experience in the workplace.
- how the 'relational' approach to IL education has, through research methods which yield exceptional detail, made possible the 'Workplace Experience Framework'. This is a guide to the structure, content and method of an evidence-based IL educational intervention, based on the range of themes and complexities of experience of IL in a workplace or profession.
- how that detail of experience can be applied to formulate a new means of monitoring an individual's IL development.

Please note: It is strongly advised that you read Chapter 2 before reading this chapter, as many of the research findings and ideas used below are introduced there and often discussed in more detail.

Introduction

In order that a professional can begin a career in the workplace using information effectively, in the context of the knowledge development and learning required for individual, team and organizational functionality, part of professional education should involve IL education of the kind appropriate for that workplace. In Chapter 8, page 111, Annemaree Lloyd suggests that students' IL development requires a transition from an academic or 'preparatory' setting to a workplace one:

> Librarians are placed in unique positions to mediate the educational and discipline/workplace landscapes in order to identify knowledge, competencies and skills that students will require while studying and when in transition to the workplace.

This chapter attempts to show one way in which workplace IL education might be based on detailed experiences of IL in the workplace, so that students are inducted into information experiences relevant to their work culture or profession. The chapter may be of particular interest to librarians attempting to develop IL in professional workers, and academics keen to develop in their students the skills that new professionals need in order to function effectively and ethically in the workplace.

In what ways has the development of IL traditionally been encouraged? Historically, the literature describes attempts to develop what are felt to be relevant skills and knowledge, based on behaviourist or constructivist approaches (Brettle, 2003 and 2007; Elrod, Wallace and Sirigos, 2012). In recent years relational IL education (Andretta, 2007) has emerged, based on knowledge of variation in IL experience, and exhibiting 'an integrated approach that facilitates the information-to-knowledge connection' (Gordon, 2009, 58).

By investigating experiences described by a representative sample of the group or profession, a study as described in Chapter 2 attempts to discover how, why and in what contexts a group or profession finds and uses information to create the subjective knowledge to function in its various roles, and what forms that knowledge takes. The current chapter discusses how, through application of the 'evidence' provided by such a study, the structure, content and learning foci of an 'evidence-based' intervention can be outlined in the form of a 'Workplace Experience Framework'. The Workplace Experience Framework, an example of which is set out below, is constructed from the range of themes, activities and ambitions which inform the experience of IL by a target group or profession. That matrix of experiences is employed, together with the Variation Theory of learning, in the development of a framework of learning contexts, aims and focal points: a framework which can be used to develop the capacity of professionals to experience IL's full range of functions within their professional, work world. By extension this would increase their potential ability to function better in their roles as well as become more likely to function effectively in higher roles in the team and organization.

The chapter concludes by showing how, in addition, such detail makes theoretically possible a method for analysing the development of IL experience, by means of a specially structured questionnaire.

Discovering the details of a profession's Information Literacy experience

The early work of Christine S. Bruce (Bruce, 1997; Bruce, Edwards and Lupton, 2006) led to the development of a 'relational' approach to IL education. That IL was experienced in a limited number of distinct ways, which varied in terms of context and complexity, suggested that IL education should be structured to take account of this. In fact, it should have as its aim the expansion of the ability to experience IL to include any and all of the ways relevant to the group or profession.

As discussed in earlier chapters, variations in experience occur due to the existence of the many knowledge development purposes for which the information is sought. Each 'purpose' may require the development of knowledge of greater or lesser complexity than others, and to fulfil several different aims within certain contexts of action described as 'themes' (Forster, 2015c). Such purposes range from the performance of simple tasks to the development of strategy and new philosophic approaches (Forster, 2015a). For any group or profession, the relationship between variations in experience is often shown to be hierarchical in this way, with the experiences arranged from least to greatest complexity (Bruce, 1997; Lloyd, 2006; Maybee, 2006; Boon, Johnston and Webber, 2007; Forster, 2015a). **With an understanding of the relevant themes and hierarchy, the educator is aware of the relevant IL experiences in the workplace that it would be valuable for the student to be capable of and facilitated into, and how they are 'related'.**

Therefore anyone interested in developing relational, evidence-based education must undertake a research study to obtain an overview of the range and hierarchy of experiences for the group or profession of interest.

As described in Chapter 2 and elsewhere, phenomenography has been used to obtain such an overview (e.g. Bruce, 1997; Limberg, 1999; Johnston and Webber, 2003; Kirk, 2004; Williams, 2007; Boon, Johnston and Webber, 2007; Lupton, 2008; Webber, Boon and Johnston, 2008; Andretta, 2010; Diehm and Lupton, 2012; Sayyad Abdi, 2014) – a methodology in which (in contrast to some methodologies such as phenomenology) variation in experience is the focus of analysis and outcome (Marton, 1988). However, only in a small number of more recent phenomenographic studies (e.g. Åkerlind, 2005; Daly, 2009; Paakkari, Tynjäläb and Kannasa, 2010; Forster, 2015a and 2015b; Wada, Backman and Forwell, 2015), of which only Forster is an investigation into IL experience, was the necessary additional detail of Dimensions of Variation and Themes of Expanding Awareness sought as described in Chapter 2. This additional detail is vital in the development of a comprehensive and effective Workplace Experience Framework, as will be shown below.

The Workplace Experience Framework

The following sections will show how we can use the IL experiences of a profession to create a 'Workplace Experience Framework' for evidence-based IL education. To begin with, we need to discuss relevant ideas of how learning occurs. The theory of learning put forward will inform the framework's structure discussed in later in this section.

A theory of learning: understanding through awareness of variations in experience

How does learning occur? Several educational psychologists in Sweden and elsewhere, using phenomenography to investigate the learning process, came to the conclusion that learning is learning to experience something in a new way for the first time (Marton and Booth, 1997). The Variation Theory of learning mentioned above, developed from the insight derived from these early studies, understands learning as *a development in the understanding of a concept through an increase in awareness of the ways it can be experienced, and hence of the variations in its meaning* (Marton and Booth, 1997; Bruce, Edwards and Lupton, 2006; Runesson, 2006; Marton and Pong, 2005).

Bruce applied this approach to Information Literacy:

> Learning is about changes in conception – teachers need to assist students in developing new and more complex ways of experiencing Information Literacy.
>
> Bruce, Edwards and Lupton, 2006, 6

Therefore there are two stages in the development of educational interventions of the Phenomenographic–Variation Theory-based type:

1. An . . . investigation into the range and variation in the experiences of a concept by particular group.
2. The application of . . . Variation Theory to the structures of data produced by that investigation, [to form the] basis for a teaching and learning programme. A programme in which the student is led to understand and experience the full range of a concept's meanings

> Åkerlind, 2008, 638

What accounts for variations in experience? Why can't everyone experience IL in all the themes and complexities that are possible in the given workplace or profession? Why are some capable of greater depth and breadth of experience of IL's knowledge-generating contexts and abilities? Variation Theory suggests that this is due to variation between individuals in *awareness* of potential contexts and roles in which the concept [such as IL] can be experienced (Marton and Booth, 1997; Åkerlind, 2008).

How is the student led to experience IL in new and more complex ways?

Matching and varying aspects of Information Literacy

Variation Theory goes on to imply that by varying the way the experience of IL is brought to a student's attention, by highlighting different relationships between its aspects, the student might come to appreciate new facets and possible contexts for information use (Runesson, 2006), and therefore potential ways of 'fitting them in' to their experiences in the future. By creating learning experiences in which students are led to think about and experience different aspects of IL in differing contextual combinations, and at varying levels of complexity, the students learn to expand their understanding of how IL can function and benefit them in their workplace.

We can use the nursing study's data (see Chapter 2) as an example. By pairing Theme 2: Relationships with patients, patients' families, colleagues and other professionals, with Theme 5: Skills and processes of evidence and other information gathering, we can produce a range of learning contexts and scenarios of varying complexity (matching different dimensions in each theme) which might focus on, for instance:

- What does it mean to relationships with other professionals and with patients and family to be able to employ a range of techniques to identify and locate information for them and to share the resulting knowledge with them in differing contexts?
- How can they facilitate the sharing of information with patients, colleagues and other professionals; the development of the trust of patients, families and colleagues; the empowerment of patients and their families; or the development of a teaching or leadership role with colleagues?

We will look at this pairing and others in more detail below.

To analyse the relationship between themes clearly, this can only be done against a background of 'invariance' in the others. Only some of the themes should be varied together in any one educational activity; the others should remain unvaried (Runesson, 2006) so that the focus of experience is sharp and clear. Our IL education intervention should be a sequence of different learning activities, each one focusing on a different pairing of themes to the exclusion of the others.

How our learning theory is applied

The structure of our Workplace Experience Framework now begins to take shape. Themes of Expanding Awareness are paired or grouped so that their varying relationships give a source of educational focus. The 'variation' is in terms of which Dimensions of Variation (level of complexity of experience of that aspect of IL) in each theme are focused on and brought in to conjunction with those of other themes.

However, which themes should be paired and why?

There are four stages of variation in a complete educational programme (Marton and Tsui, 2004). These stages when taken together make sure that variation is achieved consistently, thoroughly and appropriately for maximum educational advantage.

The first stage is **contrast.** The choice of contrast is vital. The choice of themes to form a pairing must be meaningful, and the Dimensions of Variation from the themes must be brought together in such a way as to allow the full significance of variation within these Themes to be clear. For example, varying nursing's Themes 3 and 4 together would show that the varying complexities of IL experience in the context of Evidence-Based Practice and in the development of best practice in nursing have a very significant effect on each other. Similarly Theme 3 could be varied with 5 and 6 to vividly show the contrasting effect of the varying complexity of experience of the skills and knowledge underlying effective information gathering, on the ability of IL to initiate the knowledge and knowledge-based decision-making ability needed to achieve such complex goals.

Generalization: all themes must be involved at some stage and in contrast with more than one of the others if possible. There should be sufficient range of contrasts to give a complete 'picture' of IL as experienced by our group. This helps the student recognize and contextualize their own limited experiences and (hopefully) promotes learning. As well as a full use of the themes, the variation in each theme must be completely demonstrated. For instance, in terms of the nursing study, by allowing a nurse to be made aware of all of the potential value to patients, to her team and to her own professional expertise and standing, of the adoption of more (and in some cases less) sophisticated aspects of IL experience, considerable motivation to develop that experience may be created. Generalization has a depth as well as a breadth dimension. It requires that learning materials should focus on experiences which cover the complete range of complexity within each Theme. The capacity to experience IL in these contexts can vary from the 'simple' and day-to-day to the 'strategic', depending on the demands of context. The detail possible with this analysis method gives a sure description of the nature of these variations to the advantage of educators.

Separation: this is the need to vary only *some* of the critical aspects of the phenomenon. As previously stated, this allows the features of the phenomenon to be distinguished clearly by the student. In our examples above and below only two or at most three Themes are varied together.

Fusion: this requires variation of aspects of the phenomenon to occur simultaneously to allow the relationship of the aspects, and therefore the whole structure of the phenomenon, to be made clear. Themes must be varied in pairs or threes, not individually.

The use of **contrast** and **generalization** combined with **separation** and **fusion** should provide sufficient comprehensiveness, focus and differentiation to produce learning experiences for nursing students which are likely to be effective (Åkerlind, 2008).

An example of a Workplace Experience Framework

We can now present an example of a Workplace Experience Framework. In our framework the themes are meaningfully and tellingly varied (contrast); all themes are introduced at least twice (generalization) in pairs or threes (fusion) while invariance in some themes is maintained within individual activities (separation).

After each pairing or grouping of themes there is a summary of contexts, aims and themes for learning activities based on the 'interaction' of the themes.

- Theme 2: Relationships with patients, patients' families, colleagues and other professionals and (as briefly mentioned above) Theme 5: Skills and processes of evidence and other information gathering.

Learning activities would address what it means for relationships with other professionals and with patients and family for nurses to be able to employ a range of techniques to identify and locate information for them and to share with them in differing contexts. Addressing IL in these related contexts might involve scenario work in which colleagues or patients are described in terms of their background and the information and knowledge which would empower them to make effective and confident choices about their clinical practice or their treatment. Students would be required to search for relevant information and reflect on the consequences for that person of the nurse providing or not providing relevant information, and for the student's relationship with them. Scenarios will vary in terms of the complexity of information and its potential significance to the colleague or patient – how might information support patient decision making at the simple day-to-day or at life-changing level; how might the colleague be supported, taught or led?

- Theme 3: Helping to achieve 'best practice' and Theme 4: Understandings and experiences of Evidence-based Practice.

This variation-grouping investigates the application of evidence by the nurse to her attempts to achieve the best practice possible. The latter can become more ambitious as the grasp of the role of evidence is expanded. For example, students are encouraged to see how the accumulation of a more complex evidence-based knowledge contributes to, and is necessary for, achievement of such complex goals as 'patient safety'.

- Theme 3: Helping to achieve 'best practice' with Theme 5: Skills and processes of evidence and other information gathering and Theme 6: Understanding and knowledge of the principles and concepts behind evidence and other information gathering.

This grouping would inform scenarios which aim to show the contrasting effect of complex and simple experiences and understandings of the skills and knowledge underlying effective information gathering, on the ability of IL to initiate the knowledge and knowledge-rich judgement needed to achieve the best practice possible.

- Theme 4: Understandings and experiences of Evidence-based Practice, Theme 6: Understanding and knowledge of the principles and concepts behind evidence and other information gathering and Theme 7: IL experienced through applicable conceptions of information.

This variation-grouping would examine the understanding and meaning of information and information gathering in each function of Evidence-based Practice. For example, one scenario might show how audit requires both knowledge of search strategy and of complex sources of information; what does IL mean when considered in terms of its role in audit; the varying conceptions of information used in auditing; and the principles and concepts behind locating the information types that make auditing possible? A scenario addressing simpler experiences might show how ideas about information and information gathering can affect what is regarded as valuable 'evidence'; simpler concepts of either can suggest that 'evidence' such as a patient's personal details can be easily obtained and put to valuable immediate use.

- Theme 1: Professional self-development and Theme 3: Helping to achieve 'best practice'.

This variation-grouping examines how IL has a role in the personal (ethical?)

responsibility of the nurse in various professional roles to strive for best practice, and how IL links and forms the fabric of increasingly complex and valued professional roles and best practice outcomes.

- Theme 1: Professional self-development, Theme 2: Relationships with patients, patients' families, colleagues and other professionals and Theme 7: IL experienced through applicable conceptions of information.

This grouping yields scenarios in which IL facilitates the intimate relationship between professional role and relationships with others; and how this is facilitated by understandings of different forms, roles and concepts of information, and what constitutes information: for example, information conceptualized as 'a means of understanding a newly encountered clinical problem or phenomenon', or for a nurse 'becoming able to function non-dependently within the team' while 'functioning as part of the multidisciplinary team'.

Hence all seven themes are covered.

Information professionals can base 'scenario' work on this framework, developing workshops in which the role of IL is shown through relevant examples of practice from the most to the least complexity of experience. 'Skills' training in such things as use of databases, such as Medline, can now have a meaningful context: a context which shows the real and considerable value of such skills.

Next steps

The Workplace Experience Framework is now employed to:

1 develop scenarios for learning
2 pilot-test the scenarios.

After pilot-testing scenarios which cover all of the theme groups and the varying levels of complexity expressed by the Dimensions of Variation in each pair/group, our comprehensive evidence-based educational intervention will begin to find its definitive form.

Assessing progress in Information Literacy education

This section puts forward a new method for evaluating IL capacity and development.

Finding the range of an individual's experiences of Information Literacy

The data analysis process described in Chapter 2 gave us a description of the full variation in IL experience for the group. But what can be said, in terms of this newly established framework of IL experience, about each individual's experience? To answer this question, we need to look at each transcript as a record of one person's experiences, or capacity to experience. Each participant's interview transcript must be **re-analysed to determine which of the Dimensions of Variation can be detected**. In other words, what experiences, within the themes constituting IL experience in the group or profession, are the participants currently capable of?

Each of the participants now has a detailed picture of their IL experiences in the form of Dimensions of Variation.

If the participant was interviewed again after an IL educational intervention, and the same analysis applied to the second interview transcript, might new dimensions be discovered? Thus could it be shown which themes and categories (of which the new dimensions formed part) had been reinforced? In other words, could improvement in the range and complexity of a student's ability to experience IL, and so the participant/student's educational progress, be determined? If so, a method for monitoring student IL development could be developed (Forster, 2015d).

Monitoring a student's development

The following is a description of a successful attempt to test this method; a description which also allows us to dwell on its stages in more detail. The stages are:

1   A phenomenographic study of the range of IL experiences of a profession is undertaken. A representative sample is interviewed. Interview transcripts are analysed to develop Dimensions of Variation, Themes of Expanding Awareness and Categories of Description (see Chapter 2).
2   Several of the participants have their interview transcripts re-analysed to determine which of the Dimensions of Variation were traceable in their own experiences.
3   This subgroup of participants is enrolled in an IL development module taught part-time over several months, covering contexts for: information use; range and nature of information sources; searching techniques; and critique and management of information gathered.
4   Several months after the intervention, a second interview is undertaken in which the participants are asked, in a similar way to the first

interview, about their information experiences in their working lives.

5   After the second interview, the second transcript is analysed to determine which of the (additional?) Dimensions of Variation could be detected.

Data analysis

Both transcripts were now compared. Which new dimensions were traceable in the transcript of the second interview? Could the capacity for an increased *range* of experiences of IL, indicated by new Dimensions of Variation in the second interview transcript, be determined and sensibly interpreted as theorized?

In addition, could increases in the *complexity* of the participant's experience of IL be determined and interpreted? Further insight into the effect on the participant of the module was obtained by looking at the new Dimensions of Variation from a slightly different perspective: whether each participant was able to operate at higher Categories of Description after the module?

An example from the nursing study: 'Participant D'
Dimensions of Variation from the interviews
The Dimensions of Variation shown in Tables 11.1 and 11.2 could be traced in the first and second interview transcripts. Each is numbered purely for identification purposes (see below) and appears listed under the theme of expanding awareness of which they in due course formed part.

Table 11.1 Dimensions of Variation traced in the first interview transcript

Theme 1	Theme 2	Theme 3	Theme 4	Theme 5	Theme 6	Theme 7
2	–	22, 24, 32	37, 41	48, 49	54, 57	66, 69

Table 11.2 Dimensions of Variation traced in the second interview transcript

Theme 1	Theme 2	Theme 3	Theme 4	Theme 5	Theme 6	Theme 7
2, 3, 5, 7	12, 17	20, 21, 22 23, 24, 25 27, 32, 33	37, 40	47, 49	54, 56, 57 58	63, 66, 69

Key: Information Literacy experienced in . . .

2   Establishing knowledge of, and understanding of, current practice and associate issues

3   Showing competence in day-to-day work

5   Progressing professionally. Becoming a Lifelong learner

7   Becoming able to function non-dependently within the team

12   Functioning as part of the multidisciplinary team

17   Become a patient advocate

20   Contributing evidence and other information to the multidisciplinary team

21   Determining the most cost-effective/efficient treatment option

22   Attempting to improve individual outcomes

23   Attempting to 'improve my practice'

24   Developing up-to-date practice

25   Developing objectively proven/justifiable best practice

27   Developing rationales for change

32   Focusing on the nature of patient safety

33   Achieving optimum, and so ethically defensible, care

37   Keeping up to date with the current evidence relevant to my job

40   Allowing an objective, evidentiary underpinning for practice

41   Auditing practice

47   Structuring evidence searches effectively

48   Finding all or sufficient evidence

49   Critiquing relevant evidence effectively

54   Having knowledge of correct/credible sources/databases

56   Having knowledge of database information source structure and functions

57   Having knowledge of subject headings, textwords and their use

58   Having knowledge of the structuring of searches

63   An experience of information as . . . clinical guidelines, protocols and care bundles

66   An experience of information as . . . evidence to inform practice

69   An experience of information as . . . a means to facilitate change

Compared to some other participants, there was only a moderate number of new dimensions in the second interview. The participant was one who was particularly difficult to help engage with the module.

10 of the 12 dimensions from the first interview appeared in the second. The two that didn't were 41 and 48.The reliability of the method would therefore be regarded as reasonably high from this evidence. In fact it proved to be high for the other participants also.

Theme 2 (relationships) is entirely new in the second interview and Theme 1 (professional self-development) has also been developed to some extent. Theme 3 (best practice) has been very markedly developed compared to the others. Considering the link between best practice and use of research and other evidence, perhaps development of this theme is due to, or is in a mutually supportive relationship with, the small but significant development of Theme 6, in which knowledge of the principles of evidence gathering is the focus? There was some further development in experiences in the general context of searching for appropriate evidence (Dimensions 47, 56 and 58 reinforcing 48, 49, 54, 57, 66 from the first interview). This could conceivably contribute to best practice but perhaps also, for this participant, aid in the enriching of professional competence and so a greater ability to contribute to the team – which in turn could contribute to awareness of IL's role in developing best practice.

Complexity of experiences

The Dimensions of Variation identified above are now relabelled in Tables 11.3 and 11.4 as the category of description of which they form part, to allow us to more clearly see any development in capacity for complexity of experience.

Table 11.3 Categories of Description from the first interview

Theme 1	Theme 2	Theme 3	Theme 4	Theme 5	Theme 6	Theme 7
Cat. B	–	Cat. C Cat. D Cat. F	Cat. B Cat. E	Cat. D Cat. E	Cat. A Cat. D	Cat. E Cat. F

Table 11.4 Categories of Description from the second interview

Theme 1	Theme 2	Theme 3	Theme 4	Theme 5	Theme 6	Theme 7
Cat. B Cat. C Cat. D Cat. E	Cat. C Cat. F	Cat. A Cat. B Cat. C Cat. C Cat. D Cat. D Cat. D Cat. F Cat. F	Cat. B Cat. E	Cat. C Cat. E	Cat. A Cat. C Cat. D Cat. E	Cat. C Cat. E Cat. F

Looking at each theme, and the experiences in them which are components of higher categories: two themes have Fs and three have Es in the first interview; three have Fs and four have Es in the second – only a small improvement. New Dimensions of Variation at Category F, in Contexts 2 and 3 only, suggest that IL in its role in developing the knowledge needed for ethical and patient-focused care has a relation to operating at the highest levels of awareness in professional relationships. Can it be stated as proven that complex forms of care require information-literate leadership? There is probably insufficient evidence here to back up such a statement.

Such analysis is capable of a diagnostic function and holds out the possibility of further educational interventions of a highly focused nature.

Interview . . . or questionnaire?

However, there is the apparently 'impractical' nature of the analysis methods as they stand. Interviewing each student before and after an IL course is hardly possible. Could the process be made more time- and energy-efficient by the replacement of interviews with carefully developed questionnaires based on the original analysis of variations in experience? Although phenomenography is usually an interview-based methodology, this applies to what could be described as the 'discovery' phase. Once IL experiences and their contexts are determined for the workplace or profession by an initial investigation, then a questionnaire could be employed reasonably successfully if based on them. However, the questions would not be of a 'do you do this?' type but ones of the correct phenomenographic type: 'tell me about your experiences'.

In the questionnaire students would be asked if experiences are familiar and asked to give examples. Each of the profession's experiences, in the form of a dimension of variation, would be made the subject of a question, asking for recognition of, and most importantly proof of, experiences.

The usual validity limits of 'self-reporting' would apply; however, the questions would be very focused and evidence-based and so would be more likely to stimulate memories of actual experiences. The participant could also be prepared, via preliminary communications, to reflect carefully on their experiences. A possible form of questionnaire is shown in Figure 11.1. This would make a long questionnaire. Perhaps it would be more effective if given in stages and online to make it easier to complete?

Summary

The method tested here gave enough interpretable data to suggest that the progress of students in the expansion of their capacity for experiences of varying context and complexity can be tracked and even 'measured'. Comparison of data from the two interviews allowed a detectable and significantly interpretable progression in IL development in terms of both range and complexity of experiences to be described.

In the case of some of the participants, the experiences of aspects of the phenomenon formed parts of the more complex Categories of Description. The educational intervention showed some ability to develop additional complex experience even in those participants already capable of it. However, the development was often small, which was to be expected in the IL module employed, a short, first-year undergraduate module.

In other participants, the new experiences meant that context which had not been prominent in a participant's pre-module experience became more so – especially in those themes such as Theme 6, in which skills and knowledge are the focus of experience. It could be hypothesized that experiences focused on skills and knowledge aspects of IL are 'incorporated' into experience relatively quickly in comparison to other experiences that have a more 'social' focus. Those which involved professional development and personal relationships not surprisingly showed less rapid development, but often with enough new experiences to allow developmental relationships between themes to be suggested and interpreted.

---

1. Professional Role
Tell us about experiences of using Information in ways which have supported and developed your role

Investigating newly encountered clinical conditions/situations
In what way?:

Finding out about the latest developments in clinical practice
In what way?:

Activities which led to you feeling particularly effective in your day-to-day work
In what way?:

Activities which led to you feeling confident in your role
In what way?:

Activities which helped towards progressing professionally or as part of your continuing education
In what way?:

Activities which helped you feel you were a more adaptable, flexible and responsive professional
In what way?:

Activities which helped you feel able to function non-dependently within the team
In what way?:

Activities which helped you feel you were able to be innovative in practice
In what way?:

Activities which gave you a sense of a wider professional horizon
In what way?:

Et cetera through the other Themes and their Dimensions.

Figure 11.1 *Information Literacy questionnaire*

That the detected differences can be interpreted meaningfully and plausibly in this way support the validity of this method.

Conclusion

Reproduction of the methods shown here requires the performance of a detailed research study and patient teasing out and application of its implications. However, the research, if done competently, is representative of a whole profession or other group of workers with a common information world; and therefore the Experience Framework and questionnaire, once developed, are valid for any similar group of professionals working in a similar environment. Librarians should find that once scenarios have been given additional detail and tested for practical educational value, and a relevant questionnaire has been developed and confirmed for 'reliability' in the research methodological sense (i.e. experiences described and identified in the first response to the questionnaire don't 'vanish' significantly in the second), then they can be used without additional modification whenever required.

References

ACRL (2000) *ALA/ACRL's Information Literacy Competency Standards*, www.ala.org/acrl/standards/informationliteracycompetency.

ACRL (2014) *First Part of the Draft Framework for Information Literacy for Higher Education*, http://acrl.ala.org/ilstandards/wp-content/uploads/2014/02/Framework-for-IL-for-HE-Draft-1-Part-1.pdf.

ACRL (2015) *Framework for Information Literacy for Higher Education*, www.ala.org/acrl/sites/ala.org.acrl/files/content/issues/infolit/Framework_ILHE.pdf.

Aharony, N. (2010) Information Literacy in the Professional Literature: an exploratory analysis, *Aslib Proceedings*, **62** (3), 261–82.

Åkerlind, G. S. (2005) Phenomenographic Methods: a case illustration. In Bowden, J. and Green, P. (eds), *Doing Developmental Phenomenography*, Melbourne, RMIT University Press, 103–27.

Åkerlind, G. S. (2008) A Phenomenographic Approach to Developing Academics' Understanding of the Nature of Teaching and Learning, *Teaching in Higher Education*, **13** (6), 633–44.

Åkerlind, G. S., Bowden, J. and Green, P. (2005) Learning to Do Phenomenography: a reflective discussion. In Bowden, J. and Green, P. (eds), *Doing Developmental Phenomenography*, Melbourne, RMIT University Press, 74–100.

Andretta, S. (2007) Phenomenography: a conceptual framework for information literacy education, *Aslib Proceedings: New Information Perspectives*, **59** (2), 152–68.

Andretta, S. (2009) *Transliteracy: take a walk on the wild side*, World Library and Information Congress: 75th IFLA General Conference and Assembly, Milan, Italy, 23–27 August 2009, http://eprints.rclis.org/14868/1/94-andretta-en.pdf.

Andretta, S. (2010) *Ways of Experiencing Information Literacy: perception and practice amongst Information Management postgraduate students* [Unpublished Ph.D thesis], London, Institute of Education.

Ayre, S. (2006) Workplace Based Information Skills Outreach Training to Primary Care Staff, *Health Information and Libraries Journal*, **23**, 50–4.

Baralou, E., and Tsoukas, H. (2015) How is New Organizational Knowledge Created in a Virtual Context? An ethnographic study, *Organization Studies*, **36** (5), 593–620.

Bawden, D. and Robinson, L. (2012) *Introduction to Information Science*, London, Facet Publishing.

Bonner, A. and Lloyd, A. (2011) What Information Counts at the Moment of Practice? Information practices of renal nurses, *Journal of Advanced Nursing*, **67** (6), 1213–21.

Boon, S. , Johnston, B. and Webber, S. (2007) A Phenomenographic Study of an English Faculty's Conceptions of Information Literacy, *Journal of Documentation*, **63** (2), 204–28.

Booth, S. (1997) On Phenomenography, Learning and Teaching, *Higher Education Research and Development*, **16** (2), 135–58.

Brettle, A. (2003) Information Skills Training: a systematic review of the literature, *Health Information & Libraries Journal*, **20** (Suppl 1), 3–9.

Brettle A. (2007) Evaluating Information Skills Training in Health Libraries: a systematic review, *Health Information & Libraries Journal*, **24** (Suppl 1), 18–37.

Briggs, J. (2003) *Aligning Teaching and Assessment to Curriculum Objectives*, London, Higher Education Academy, www.heacademy.ac.uk/resources/detail/resource_database/id477_aligning_ teaching_for_constructing_learning.

Brody, R. (2008) The Problem of Information Naïveté, *Journal of the American Society for Information Science and Technology*, **59** (7), 1124–7.

Brown, J. S., Collins, A. and Duguid, P. (1989) Situated Cognition and the Culture of Learning, *Educational Researcher*, **18** (1), 32–42.

Browning, S. (2015) 'Data, Data, Everywhere, Nor Any Time to Think: DIY analysis of e-resource access problems, *Journal of Electronic Resources Librarianship*, **27** (1), 26–34.

Browning, S. (2016) The Discovery-collection Librarian Connection: cultivating collaboration for better discovery, *Collection Management*, **40** (4), 197–206.

Bruce, C. S. (1997) *Seven Faces of Information Literacy*, Adelaide, Auslib Press.

Bruce, C. S. (1998) The Phenomenon of Information Literacy, *Higher Education Research and Development*, **17** (1), 25–44.

Bruce, C. S. (1999) Workplace Experience of Information Literacy, *International Journal of Information Management*, **19**, 33–47.

Bruce, C. S. (2000) Information Literacy Research: dimensions of the emerging collective consciousness, *Academic and Research Libraries*, **31** (2), 91–109.

Bruce, C. S. (2002) *Information Literacy as a Catalyst for Educational Change: a background paper*, Prague, US National Commission on Libraries and Information Science & the National Forum on Information Literacy, http://eprints.qut.edu.au/4977/1/4977_1.pdf.

Bruce, C. S. (2008) *Informed Learning*, Chicago, IL, Association of College & Research Libraries/American Library Association.

Bruce, C. S. (2012) *Education, Research, and Information Services* [workshop presentation], Auraria Library, University of Colorado, Denver, CO (unpublished).

Bruce, C. S. (2013) Keynote address: Information Literacy Research and Practice, an Experiential Perspective. In Kurbanoglu, S., Grassian, E., Mizrachi, D., Catts, R. and Spiranec, S. (eds), *Worldwide Commonalities and Challenges in Information Literacy Research and Practices: European Conference on Information Literacy*, revised selected papers, Communications in Computer and Information Science Series Vol. 397, Heidelberg, NY, Springer, 11–30.

Bruce, C. S. and Hughes, H. (2010) Informed Learning: a pedagogical construct connecting information and learning, *Library and Information Science Research*, **32** (4), A2–A8.

Bruce, C. S., Edwards, S. and Lupton, M. (2006) Six Frames for Information Literacy Education: a conceptual framework for interpreting the relationships between theory and practice, *Italics*, **5** (1), 1–18.

Bruce, C. S., Hughes, H. and Somerville, M. M. (2012) Supporting Informed Learners in the 21st century, *Library Trends*, **60** (3), 522–45.

Bruce, C. S., Somerville, M. M., Stoodley, I. and Partridge, H. (2014) Diversifying Information Literacy Research: an Informed Learning perspective. In Bruce, C., Davis, K., Hughes, H., Partridge, H. and Stoodley, I. (eds), *Information Experience: approaches to theory and practice*, London, Emerald, 169–89.

Cambridge English Dictionary (2016) Definition: 'Profession', http://dictionary.cambridge.org/dictionary/english/profession.

Cerbone, D. R. (2006) *Understanding Phenomenology*, Durham, Acumen.

Checkland, P. and Holwell, S. (1998) *Information, Systems, and Information Systems: making sense of the field*, Chichester, John Wiley & Sons.

Checkland, P. B. and Poulter, J. (2006) *Learning for Action: a short definitive account of soft systems methodology and its use for practitioners, teachers, and students*, Chichester, John Wiley.

Cheuk, B. (1998) An Information Seeking and Using Process Model in the Workplace: a constructivist approach, *Asian Libraries*, **7** (12), 375–90.

Cheuk, B. (2002) *Information Literacy in the Workplace Context: issues, best practices and challenges*, White paper prepared for UNESCO, the US National Commission on Libraries and Information Science and the National Forum on Information Literacy, for use at the Information Literacy Meeting of Experts, Prague, Czech Republic.

Cheuk, B. (2008) Delivering Business Value Through Information Literacy in the Workplace, *Libri*, **58** (3), 137–43.

Cheuk, B. (2016) *Making Sense of Social Collaboration, Leadership 2.0 and Future of Work. Social Now Europe 2016 Keynote Presentation, slide 11*, www.slideshare.net/BonnieCheuk/social-now-europe-2016-bonnie-cheuk-keynote-presentation-making-sense-of-social-collaboration-leadership-20-and-future-of-work.

Cheuk, B. and Dervin, B. (2011) Leadership 2.0 in Action: a journey from knowledge management to 'knowledging', *Knowledge Management & E-Learning: an International Journal (KM&EL)*, **3** (2), 119–38.

Conley, T. and Gill, E. (2011) Information Literacy for Undergraduate Business Students: examining value, relevancy and implications for the new century, *Journal of Business and Finance Librarianship*, **16**, 213–28.

Costas, J. (2013) Problematizing Mobility: a metaphor of stickiness, non-places and the kinetic elite, *Organisation Studies*, **34** (10), 1467–85.

Crawford, J. and Irving, C. (2009) Information Literacy in the Workplace: a qualitative exploratory study, *Journal of Librarianship and Information Science*, **41** (1), 29–38.

Crossan, M. M., Lane, H. W. and White, R. E. (1999) An Organizational Learning Framework: from intuition to institution, *Academy of Management Review*, **24**, 522–37.

Daly, S. (2009) *The Design Landscape: a phenomenographic study of design experiences*, ASEE Annual Conference and Exposition.

de Saulles, M. (2007) Information Literacy Amongst UK SMEs: an information policy gap, *Aslib Proceedings*, **59** (1), 68–79.

Dervin, B. (2003) *Sense-Making Methodology Reader: selected writings of Brenda Dervin* (Communication Alternatives), New York, NY, Hampton Press.

Diehm, R. and Lupton, M. (2012) Approaches to Learning Information Literacy: a phenomenographic study, *Journal of Academic Librarianship*, **38** (4), 217–25.

Dixon, K. R. and Panteli, N. (2010) From Virtual Teams to Virtuality in Teams, *Human Relations*, **63** (8), 1177–97.

Doyle, C. S. (1992) *Outcome Measures for Information Literacy within the National Education Goals of 1990*, Final report to National Forum on Information Literacy, Syracuse, NY, ERIC.

Eaton, J. J. and Bawden, D. (1991) What Kind of Resource is Information?, *International Journal of Information Management*, **11** (2), 156–65.

Elrod, R. E., Wallace, E. D. and Sirigos, C. B. (2012) Teaching Information Literacy: a review of 100 syllabi, *Southeastern Librarian*, **60** (3), 8–15.

Eraut, M. (1994) *Developing Professional Knowledge and Competence*, London, Routledge Falmer.

European Commission (2016) *Digital Skills at the Core of the New Skills Agenda for Europe*, https://ec.europa.eu/digital-single-market/en/news/digital-skills-core-new-skills-agenda-europe.

Evetts, J. (2006) The Sociology of the Professions, *Current Sociology*, **54** (1), 133–43.

Fenwick, T. (2013) Understanding Transitions in Professional Practice and Learning: towards new questions for research, *Journal of Workplace Learning*, **25** (6), 352–67.

Fister, B. (2015) *A Bit of a Tall Order, Inside Higher Education*, Library Babel Fish, www.insidehighered.com/blogs/library-babel-fish/%E2%80%9C-bit-tall-order%E2%80%9D.

Floridi, L. (2010) *Information: a very short introduction*, Oxford, Oxford University Press.

Ford, N. (2004) Towards a Model of Learning for Educational Informatics, *Journal of Documentation*, **60** (2), 183–225.

Ford, N. (2008) Educational Informatics, *Annual Review of Information Science and Technology*, **42** (1), 497–544.

Forster, M. (2013) Information Literacy as a Facilitator of Ethical Practice in the Professions, *Journal of Information Literacy*, **7** (1), 18–29.

Forster, M. (2015a) 6 Ways Of Experiencing Information Literacy In Nursing – The Findings of a Phenomenographic Study, *Nurse Education Today*, **35** (1), 195–200.

Forster, M. (2015b) Phenomenography: a methodology for information literacy research, *Journal of Librarianship & Information Science*, DOI 10.11770961000614566481.

Forster, M. (2015c) Refining the Definition of Information Literacy: the experience of contextual knowledge creation, *Journal of Information Literacy*, **9** (1), 62–73.

Forster , M. (2015d) *An Investigation into Information Literacy in Nursing Practice – how is it experienced, what are its parameters, and how can it be developed?* [Doctoral thesis], University of West London.

Freudenberg, B. (2008) *Learning to Learn: business professionals' perceptions of information literacy*, ConTax Student e-Newsletter, www.taxinstitute.com.au/images/contax/ConTax_Apr08_Feature_Article.pdf.

Gambrill, E. (2007) Views of Evidence-based Practice: social workers' code of ethics and accreditation standards as guides for choice, *Journal of Social Work Education*, **43** (3), 447–62.

Garrison, D. R. (2014) Community of Inquiry. In Coghlan, D. and Brydon-Miller, M. (eds), *The SAGE Encyclopedia of Action Research*, Vol. 1, Los Angeles, CA, SAGE Reference, 147–50.

Gashirpv, I. and Matsuucki, G. (2013) CUNY's Critical Thinking Skills Initiative: resdesigning workforce education through information literacy learning, *College & Research Libraries News*, **74** (2), 70–3.

Gasteen, G. and O'Sullivan C. (2000) Working Towards an Information Literate Law Firm. In Bruce, C. and Candy, P. (eds), *Information Literacy Around the World: advances in programs and research*, Wagga Wagga, Centre for Information Studies, Charles Sturt University, 109–20.

General Social Care Council (GSCC) (2010) *Codes of Practice for Social Care Workers*, http://webarchive.nationalarchives.gov.uk/20120708184859/ http://www.gscc.org.uk/cmsFiles/CodesofPracticeforSocialCareWorkers.pdf.

Gherardi, S. (2009a) Practice? It's a matter of taste, *Management Learning*, **40** (5), 535–50.

Gherardi, S. (2009b) Knowing and Learning in Practice-based Studies: an introduction, *The Learning Organization*, **16** (5), 352–9.

Glasper, E. A. (2011) The RCN's Information Literacy Competences for Evidence-based Practice, *British Journal of Nursing*, **20** (3), 188–9.

Goad, T. W. (2002) *Information Literacy and Workplace Performance*, London, Quorum Books.

Goldstein, S. (2014) *Transferring Information Know-how: information literacy at the interface between higher education and employment*, www.researchinfonet.org/wp-content/uploads/2014/09/Report-on-transferability-of-ILbeyond-academia-FINAL.pdf.

Goldstein, S. and Whitworth, A. (2014) *DeVIL – Determining the Value of Information Literacy for Employers*, www.informall.org.uk/wp-content/uploads/2015/11/DeVIL_report_final_draft_v05.pdf.

Gordon, C. A. (2009) An Emerging Theory for Evidence Based Information Literacy Instruction in School Libraries, Part 1: building a foundation, *Evidence Based Library & Information Practice*, **4** (2), 56–77.

Granovetter, M. (1973) The Strength of Weak Ties, *American Journal of Sociology*, **78**, 1360–80.

Green, B. (ed.) (2009) *Understanding and Researching Professional Practice*, Rotterdam, Sense Publishers.

Grieves, M. (1998) The Impact of Information Use on Decision Making: studies in five sectors – introduction, summary and conclusions, *Library Management*, **19** (2), 78–85.

Hager, P. (2004) Conceptions of Learning and Understanding Learning at Work, *Studies in Continuing Education*, **26** (1), 3–17.

Hallam, G., Hiskens, A. and Ong, R. (2014) Conceptualising the Learning Organisation: creating a maturity framework to develop a shared understanding of the library's role in learning and literacy, *Australian Library Journal*, **63** (2), 78–93.

Harmer, B. M. and Pauleen, D. J. (2012) Attitude, Aptitude, Ability and Autonomy: the emergence of 'offroaders': a special class of nomadic workers, *Behaviour & Information Technology*, **31** (5), 439.

Harris, B. R. (2008) Communities as Necessity in Information Literacy Development: challenging the standards, *Journal of Academic Librarianship*, **34** (3), 248–55.

Hatala, J-P. and Lutta, J. G. (2009) Managing Information Sharing Within an Organizational Setting: a social network perspective, *Performance Improvement Quarterly*, **21** (4) 5–33.

Head, A. (2012) *How College Graduates Solve Information Problems Once They Join The Workplace*, Project Information Literacy Research Report. The Passage Studies, https://library.educause.edu/resources/2012/10/learning-curve-how-college-graduates-solve-information-problems-once-they-join-the-workplace.

Heichman Taylor, L. (2008) Information Literacy in Subject-specific Vocabularies:

a path to critical thinking, *College and Undergraduate Libraries*, **15**, 141–58.

Hepworth, M. and Smith, M. (2008) Workplace Information Literacy for Administrative Staff in HE, *Australian Library Journal*, **57** (3), 212–36.

Hepworth, M. and Walton, G. (eds) (2013) *Developing People's Information Capabilities: fostering information literacy in educational, workplace and community contexts*, Bingley, Emerald Group.

Herrington, J. (2006) *Authentic E-learning in Higher Education: design principles for authentic learning environments and tasks*, http://ro.uow.edu.au/cgi/viewcontent.cgi?article=1029&context=edupapers.

Hjørland, B. (2000) Information Seeking Behavior: what should a general theory look like, *New Review of Information Behaviour Research*, **1**, 19–33.

Howe, C. D. (2012) Undergraduate Information Literacy Instruction is Not Enough to Prepare Junior Doctors for Evidence-based Practice, *Evidence Based Library & Information Practice*, **7** (2), 76–8.

Hoyt, R. E., Bailey, N. and Yoshihashi, A. (2012) *Health Informatics: practical guide for healthcare and information technology professionals*, 5th edn, Raleigh, NC, Lulu.

Hughes, H. (2014) Researching Information Experience: methodological snapshots. In Bruce, C., Partridge, H., Hughes, H., Davis, K. and Stoodley, I. (eds), *Information Experience: approaches to theory and practice*. Bingley, Emerald, 33–50.

Inskip, C. (2014) *Information Literacy is for Life, Not Just for a Good Degree: a literature review*, London, CILIP.

Johnston, B. and Webber, S. (2003) Information Literacy in Higher Education: a review and case study, *Studies in Higher Education*, **28** (3), 335–52.

Kemmis, S. and Grootenboer, P. (2008) Situating Praxis in Practice: practice architectures and the cultural, social and material conditions for practice. In Kemmis, S. and Smith, T. (eds), *Enabling Praxis: challenges for education*, Rotterdam, Sense Publishers, 37–62.

Kirk, J. (2004) *Information and Work: extending the roles of information professionals*, paper presented at the Challenging Ideas, ALIA 2004 Biennial Conference, Gold Coast, QLD, www.conferences.alia.org.au/alia2004/pdfs/kirk.j.paper.pdf.

Kitchener, K. S. (2000) *Foundations of Ethical Practice, Research, and Teaching in Psychology*, Mahwah, NJ, Lawrence Erlbaum.

Koufogiannakis, D. (2013) Academic Librarians Use Evidence for Convincing, *SAGE Open*, **3** (2), 1–12.

Kuhlthau, C. C. (1988) Developing a Model of the Library Search Process: cognitive and affective aspects, *RQ*, **28** (2), 232–42.

Kuhlthau, C. C. (2004) *Seeking Meaning: a process approach to library and information services*, 2nd edn, Westport, CT, Libraries Unlimited.

Lave, J. and Wenger, E. (1991) *Situated Learning: legitimate peripheral participation*, Series: Learning in Doing: Social, Cognitive and Computational Perspectives, Cambridge, Cambridge University Press.

Law Society (2016) *Continuing Competence Guidance – FAQs*,

www.lawsociety.org.uk/support-services/advice/articles/continuing-competence-guidance-faqs.

Leavitt, L. L. (2011) 21st Century Workforce Initiatives: implications for information literacy instruction in academic libraries, *Education Libraries*, **34** (2), 15–18.

Levy, P. and Roberts, S. (eds) (2005) *Developing the New Learning Environment: the changing role of the academic librarian*, London, Facet Publishing.

Limberg, L. (1999) Three Conceptions of Information Seeking and Use. In Wilson, T. D. and Allen, D. K. (eds), *Exploring the Contexts of Information Behaviour*, London, Taylor and Graham, 116–35.

Limberg, L. and Sundin, O. (2006) Teaching Information Seeking: relating information literacy education to theories of information behaviour, *Information Research*, **12** (1), paper 280, http://InformationR.net/ir/12-1/paper280.html.

Lloyd, A. (2003) Information Literacy the Meta-competency of the Knowledge Economy? An exploratory paper, *Journal of Librarianship and Information Science*, **35** (2), 87–92.

Lloyd, A. (2005) Information Literacy: different contexts, different concepts, different truths?, *Journal of Librarianship and Information Science*, **37** (2), 82–8.

Lloyd, A. (2006) Information Literacy Landscapes: an emerging picture, *Journal of Documentation*, **62** (5), 570–83.

Lloyd, A. (2007) Recasting Information Literacy as Socio-cultural Practices: implications for library and information science researchers, *Information Research*, **12** (4), 1–13.

Lloyd, A. (2009) Informing Practice: information experiences of ambulance officers in training and on-road practice, *Journal of Documentation*, **65** (3), 396–419.

Lloyd, A. (2010) *Information Literacy Landscapes: information literacy in education, workplace and everyday contexts*, London, Elsevier.

Lloyd, A. (2012) Information Literacy as a Socially Enacted Practice: sensitising themes for an emerging perspective of people-in-practice, *Journal of Documentation*, **68** (6), 772–83.

Lloyd, A. (2013) Building Information Resilient Workers: the critical ground of workplace information literacy: what have we learnt? In *Worldwide Commonalities and Challenges in Information Literacy Research and Practice*, New York, NY, Springer, 219–28.

Lloyd, A. (2014) Building Information Resilience: how do resettling refugees connect with health information in regional landscapes – implications for health literacy, *Australian Academic & Research Libraries*, **45** (1), 48–66.

Lloyd, A. and Williamson, K. (2008) Towards an Understanding of Information Literacy in Context: implications for research, *Journal of Librarianship and Information Science*, **40** (1), 3–12.

Lo, M. (2012) *Variation Theory and the Improvement of Teaching and Learning*, Gothenburg, Göteborgs Universitet.

Lombard, E. (2010) *Pursuing Information Literacy: roles and relationships*, Witney, Chandos Publishing.

Loo, J. L. and Dupois, E. A. (2015) Organizational Learning for Library Enhancements: a collaborative, research-driven analysis of academic department needs, *College & Research Libraries*, **76** (5), 671–89.

Lundh, A. and Alexandersson, M. (2012) Collecting and Compiling: the activity of seeking pictures in primary school, *Journal of Documentation*, **68** (2), 238–53.

Lupton, M. (2004) *The Learning Connection: information literacy and the student experience*, Adelaide, Auslib Press.

Lupton, M. (2008) Evidence, Argument and Social Responsibility: researching an essay, *Higher Education Research and Development*, **27** (4), 399–414.

Macoustra, J. (2004) Information Literacy: organisational and law firm perspectives, *Legal Information Management*, **4**, 130–5.

Martin, J. (2013) Refreshing Information Literacy: learning from recent British information literacy models, *Communications in Information Literacy*, **7** (2), 114.

Marton, F. (1988) Phenomenography: a research approach to investigating different understandings of reality. In Sherman, R. R. and Webb, R. B. (eds), *Qualitative Research in Education: focus and methods*, London, Routledge Falmer, 141–61.

Marton, F. (1994) Phenomenography. In Husen, T. and Postlethwaite, T. N. (eds), *International Encyclopedia of Education*, Vol. 8, 2nd edn, London, Pergamon, 4424–9.

Marton, F. and Booth, S. (1997) *Learning and Awareness*, Hillsdale, NJ, Lawrence Erlbaum.

Marton, F. and Pong, W. Y. (2005) On the Unit of Description in Phenomenography, *Higher Education Research and Development*, **24**, 335–48.

Marton, F. and Tsui, A. (2004) *Classroom Discourse and the Space of Learning*, Hillsdale, NJ, Lawrence Erlbaum.

Materska, K. (2013) Is Information Literacy Enough for a Knowledge Worker? In Kurbanoglu, S., Grassian, E., Mizrachi, D., Catts, R. and Spiranec, S. (eds), *Worldwide Commonalities and Challenges in Information Literacy Research and Practices: European Conference on Information Literacy*, revised selected papers, Communications in Computer and Information Science Series Vol. 397, Heidelberg, NY, Springer, 229–35.

Maybee, C. (2006) Undergraduate Perceptions of Information Use: the basis for creating user-centered student information literacy instruction, *Journal of Academic Librarianship*, **32** (1), 79–85.

Megill, K. A. (2012) *Thinking for a Living: the coming age of knowledge work*, Boston, MA, Walter De Gruyter.

Merriam-Webster (n.d.). Definition: 'Profession', www.merriam-webster.com/dictionary/profession.

Mirijamdotter, A. (2010) Toward Collaborative Evidence Based Information Practices: organisation and leadership essentials, *Evidence Based Library and Information Practice*, **5** (1), 17–25.

Mirijamdotter, A. (2015) Auraria Library Report on Communication Systems. In *Informed Systems: organizational design for learning in action*, Oxford, Chandos Publishing, 151–63.

Mirijamdotter, A. and Somerville, M. M. (2009) Collaborative Design: an SSM-enabled organizational learning approach, *International Journal of Information Technologies and Systems Approach*, **2** (1), 48–69.

Moore, G. A. (2015) *Zone to Win: organizing to compete in an age of disruption*, New York, NY, Diversion Books.

Mutch, A. (2008) *Managing information and Knowledge in Organizations: a literacy approach*, London, Taylor & Francis.

National Forum on Information Literacy (n.d.) *Workplace Information Literacy*, http://infolit.org/workplace-information-literacy.

Nicholas, D. and Rowlands, I. (eds) (2008) *Digital Consumers*, London, Facet Publishing.

Nonaka, I. (1994) A Dynamic Theory of Organizational Knowledge Creation, *Organization Science*, **5** (1), 14–37.

Nonaka, I. (2007) The Knowledge Creating Company, *Harvard Business Review*, **85**, 162–71.

Nursing and Midwifery Council (NMC) (2010) *The Code: standards of conduct, performance and ethics for nurses and midwives*, www.nmc-uk.org/Publications/Standards/The-code/Introduction.

O'Farrill, R. T. (2008) *Conceptions of Effective Information Use and Learning in a Tele-Health Organization: a phenomenographic study of information literacy and knowledge management at work*, Aberdeen, The Robert Gordon University (unpublished PhD thesis).

O'Farrill, R. T. (2010) Information Literacy and Knowledge Management at Work: conceptions of effective information use at NHS24, *Journal of Documentation*, **66** (5), 706–33.

O'Sullivan, C. (2002) Is Information Literacy Relevant in the Real World?, *Reference Services Review*, **30** (1), 7–14.

Oliver, G. (2011) *Organisational Culture for Information Managers*, Oxford, Chandos Publishing.

Orlikowski, W. J. (2007) Sociomaterial practices: exploring technology at work, *Organization Studies*, **28** (9), 1435–48.

Osborn, A. (2011) *The Value of Information Literacy: conceptions of BSc Nursing students at a UK university*, University of Huddersfield (unpublished PhD thesis).

Ouye, J. A. (2011) *Five Trends that are Dramatically Changing Work and the Workplace*, www.knoll.com/media/18/144/WP_FiveTrends.pdf.

Paakkari, L., Tynjäläb, P. and Kannasa, L. (2010) Student Teachers' Ways of Experiencing the Objective of Health Education as a School Subject: a phenomenographic study, *Teaching and Teacher Education*, **26** (4), 941–8.

Pan, D. and Howard, Z. (2009) Reorganizing a Technical Services Division Using

Collaborative Evidence-based Information Practice at Auraria Library, *Evidence Based Library and Information Practice*, **4** (4), 88–94.

Pan, D. and Howard, Z. (2010) Distributing Leadership and Cultivating Dialogue with Collaborative EBIP, *Library Management*, **31** (7), 494–504.

Pan, D., Bradbeer, G. and Jurries, E. (2011) From Communication to Collaboration: blogging to troubleshoot e-resources, *The Electronic Library*, **29** (3), 344–53.

Pang, M. and Marton, F. (2003) Beyond 'Lesson Study': comparing two ways of facilitating the grasp of some economic concepts, *Instructional Science*, **31** (3), 175–94.

Partridge, H., Edwards, S. and Thorpe, C. (2010) Evidence-based Practice: information professionals' experience of information literacy in the workplace. In Partridge, H., Edwards, S., Clare, T., Lloyd, A. and Taljo, S. (eds), *Practising Information Literacy: bringing theories of learning, practice and information literacy together*, Wagga Wagga, Centre for Information Studies, Charles Sturt University, 273–98.

Perrault, A. M. (2007) *American Competitiveness in the Internet Age: information literacy summit*, http://infolit.org/wp-content/uploads/2012/09/Summit16Oct2007B.pdf.

Pilerot, O. (2016) A Practice-based Exploration of the Enactment of Information Literacy among PhD Students in an Interdisciplinary Research Field, *Journal of Documentation*, **72** (3), 414–34.

Poirier, L. and Robinson, L. (2014) Informational Balance: slow principles in the theory and practice of information behaviour, *Journal of Documentation*, **70** (4), 687–707.

Professions Australia (n.d.) *What is a Profession?*, www.professions.com.au/about-us/what-is-a-professional.

Ramsden, P. (1988) Studying Learning: improving teaching. In Ramsden, P. (ed.), *Improving Learning New Perspectives* London, Kogan Page, 13–33.

Reich, A. and Hager, P. (2014) Problematising Practice, Learning and Change: practice-theory perspectives on professional learning, *Journal of Workplace Learning*, **26** (6/7), 418–31.

Roach, M. S. (1992) *The Human Act of Caring*, Ottawa, Canadian Hospital Association.

Roberts, S. A. (2002) Knowledge and Corporate Communication. In *Proceedings of Conference On Corporate Communication: communication renewal*, Wroxton, 30 June–3 July 2002, 168–81.

Roberts, S. A. (2004) Knowledge Management for Best Practice. In Oliver, S. (ed.), *Handbook of Corporate Communication and Public Relations: pure and applied*, London, Routledge, 34–53.

Runesson, U. (2006) What is it Possible to Learn? On variation as a necessary condition for learning, *Scandinavian Journal of Educational Research*, **50** (4), 397–410.

Sackett, D. L., Richardson, S. R., Rosenberg, W. and Haynes, R. B. (1997) *Evidence Based Medicine: how to practice and teach EBM*, Edinburgh, Churchill Livingstone.

Sayyad Abdi, E. (2014) *Web Professionals: how do they experience information literacy?* PhD thesis, Queensland University of Technology.

Sayyad Abdi, E. and Bruce, C. S. (2015) From Workplace to Profession: new focus for the information literacy discourse. In *Information Literacy: moving toward sustainability*, Communications in Computer and Information Science, Vol. 552, 59–69.

Sayyad Abdi, E., Partridge, H. and Bruce, C. (2016) Web Designers and Developers Experiences of Information Literacy: a phenomenographic study, *Library & Information Science Research*, **38** (4), 353–9.

SCONUL (2011) *SCONUL Seven Pillars of Information Literacy*, www.sconul.ac.uk/groups/information_literacy/papers/Seven_pillars2.pdf.

Schatzki, T. R. (1996) *Social Practices: a Wittgensteinian approach to human activity and the social*, Cambridge, Cambridge University Press.

Schatzki, T. R. (2002) *The Site of the Social: a philosophical exploration of the constitution of social life and change*, Pennsylvania, Pennsylvania State University Press.

Schön, D. (1983) *The Reflective Practitioner — How Professionals Think in Action*, New York, NY, Basic Books.

Secker, J. (2012) Digital Literacy Support for Researchers: the personalised approach. In Priestner, A. and Tilley, E. (eds), *Personalising Library Services in Higher Education: the boutique approach*, Farnham, Ashgate, 107–25.

Secker, J. and Coonan, E. (2011) *A New Curriculum for Information Literacy*, Arcadia project, Cambridge University Library.

Secker, J. and Coonan, E. (2013) *Rethinking Information Literacy: a practical framework for supporting learning*, London, Facet Publishing.

Secker, J. and Morrison, C. (2016) From Anxiety to Empowerment: supporting librarians develop copyright literacy, *ALISS Quarterly*, **12** (1), 10–13.

Sen, B. A. and Taylor, R. (2007) Determining the Information Needs of Small and Medium-sized Enterprises: a critical success factor analysis, *Information Research*, **12** (4), 1.

Senge, P. (1990) *The Fifth Discipline: the art and practice of the learning organization*, London, Century.

Senge, P. (1999) *The Dance of Change: the challenges to sustaining momentum in a learning organization*, New York, NY, Doubleday.

Sennett, R. (2007) *The Culture of the New Capitalism*, New Haven, CT, Yale University Press.

Shove, E., Pantzar, M. and Watson, M. (2012) *The Dynamics of Social Practice: everyday life and how it changes*, London, Sage Publications.

Shu, Q., Tu, Q. and Wang, K. (2011) The Impact of Computer Self-efficacy and Technology Dependence on Computer-related Technostress: a social cognitive theory perspective, *International Journal of Human-Computer Interaction*, **27** (10), 923–39.

Skyrius, R. and Bujauskas, V. (2010) A Study on Complex Information Needs in Business Activities, *Informing Science: the International Journal of an Emerging Transdiscipline*, **13**, 1–13.

Smith, N. M. and Presser, P. (2005) Embed with the Faculty: legal information skills online, *Journal of Academic Librarianship*, **31** (3), 247–62.

Smith, M. and Trede, F. (2013) Reflective Practice in the Transition Phase from University Student to Novice Graduate: implications for teaching reflective practice, *Higher Education Research & Development*, **32** (4), 632–45.

Snavely, L. and Cooper, N. (1997) The Information Literacy Debate, *Journal of Academic Librarianship*, **23** (1), 9–20.

Snowden, D. J. and Boone, M. E. (2007) A Leader's Framework for Decision Making, *Harvard Business Review*, **85** (11), 68–76.

Somerville, M. M. (2009) *Working Together: collaborative information practices for organizational learning*, Chicago, IL, Association of College & Research Libraries/American Library Association.

Somerville, M. M. (2013) Digital Age Discoverability: a collaborative organizational approach, *Serials Review*, **39** (4), 234–39.

Somerville, M. M. (2015a) *Informed Systems: organizational design for learning in action*, Oxford, Chandos Publishing.

Somerville, M. M. (2015b) Information, Information Systems, and Information Technology: vital elements for transformative organizational learning, Guest lecture in 'Introduction to informatics' graduate course in Information Systems, Linnaeus University, Växjö, Sweden.

Somerville, M. M. and Brown-Sica, M. (2011) Library Space Planning: a participatory action research approach, *The Electronic Library*, **29** (5), 669–81.

Somerville, M. M. and Chatzipanagiotou, N. (2015) Informed Systems: enabling collaborative evidence based organizational learning, *Evidence Based Library and Information Practice*, **10** (4), http://ejournals.library.ualberta.ca/index.php/EBLIP/article/view/25326.

Somerville, M. M. and Farner, M. (2012) Appreciative Inquiry: a transformative approach for initiating shared leadership and organizational learning, *Revista de Cercetare si Interventie Sociala [Review of Research and Social Intervention]*, special issue on appreciative Inquiry and social practice, **38** (September), 7–24, www.rcis.ro.

Somerville, M. M. and Howard, Z. (2010) Information in Context: co-designing workplace structures and systems for organisational learning, *Information Research*, **15** (4), paper 446, http://InformationR.net/ir/15–4/paper446.html.

Somerville, M. M. and Kloda, L. (2016) Academic Libraries. In Brettle, A. and Koufogiannakis, D. (eds), *Being Evidence Based in Library and Information Practice*, London, Facet Publishing, 93–104.

Somerville, M. M. and Mirijamdotter, A. (2014) Information Experiences in the Workplace: foundations for an informed systems approach. In Bruce, C., Davis, K., Hughes, H., Partridge, H. and Stoodley, I. (eds), *Information Experience: approaches to theory and practice*, London, Emerald, 203–20.

Somerville, M. M., Mirijamdotter, A., Bruce, C. S. and Farner, M. (2014) Informed

Systems Approach: new directions for organizational learning. In Jaabæk, M. and Gjengstø, H. (eds), *International Conference on Organizational Learning, Knowledge and Capabilities* (OLKC 2014: Circuits of Knowledge), Oslo, BI Norwegian Business School, www.divaportal.org/smash/get/diva2:714317/FULLTEXT02.pdf.

Somerville, M. M., Rogers, E., Mirijamdotter, A. and Partridge, H. (2007) Collaborative Evidence-based Information Practice: the Cal Poly digital learning initiative. In Connor, E. (ed.), *Evidence-Based Librarianship: case studies and active learning exercises*, Oxford, Chandos Publishing, 141–61.

Somerville, M. M., Schader, B. and Huston, M. E. (2005) Rethinking What We Do and How We Do It: systems thinking strategies for library leadership, *Australian Academic and Research Libraries*, **36** (4), 214–27.

Streatfield, D. and Markless, S. (2008) Evaluating the Impact of Information Literacy in Higher Education: progress and prospects, *Libri*, **58** (2), 102–9.

Swales, J. M. (1990) *Genre Analysis: English in academic and research settings*, Cambridge, Cambridge University Press.

Tagliaventi, M. and Mattarelli, E. (2006) The Role of Networks of Practice, Value Sharing, and Operational Proximity in Knowledge Flows Between Professional Groups, *Human Relations*, **59** (3), 291–319.

Todd, R. J. (1995) Integrated Information Skills Instruction: does it make a difference?, *School Library Media Quarterly*, **23** (2), 133–8.

Townsend, A. (2014) Collaborative Action Research. In Coghlan, D. and Brydon-Miller, M. (eds), *The SAGE Encyclopedia of Action Research*, Vol. 1, Thousand Oaks, CA, SAGE, 116–19.

Travis, T. (2011) From the Classroom to the Boardroom: the impact of information literacy instruction on workplace research skills, *Education Libraries*, **34** (2), 19–31.

Wada, M., Backman, C. L. and Forwell, S. J. (2015) Men's Discursive Constructions of Balance in Everyday Life, *Community Work & Family*, **18** (1), 117–33.

Webber, S., Boon, S. and Johnston, B. (2008) *Variation Theory as a Basis for Designing a Module on Teaching Information Literacy*, SIG Phenomenography Conference, Kristianstad, Sweden, 22 May 2008, www.slideshare.net/sheilawebber/variation-theory-as-a-basis-for-designing-a-module-on-teaching-information-literacy.

Weiner, S. (2011) How Information Literacy Becomes Policy: an analysis using the multiple streams framework, *Library Trends*, **60** (2), 297–311.

Wenger, E. (1998) *Communities of Practice: learning, meaning and identity*, Cambridge, Cambridge University Press.

Wenger, E., White, N. and Smith, J. (2009) *Digital Habitats: stewarding technology for communities*, Portland, OR, CPSquare.

White, M. (2012) Digital Workplaces: vision and reality, *Business Information Review*, **29** (4), 205–14.

Whitworth, A. (2014) *Radical Information Literacy: reclaiming the political heart of the IL movement,* Oxford, Chandos Publishing.

Williams, D. (2007) Secondary School Teachers' Conceptions of Information Literacy, *Journal of Librarianship and Information Science,* **39** (4), 199–212.

Williams, D., Cooper, K. and Wavell, C. (2014) *Information Literacy in the Workplace: an annotated bibliography,* Aberdeen, Robert Gordon University.

Yates, C., Partridge, H. L. and Bruce, C. S. (2009) Learning Wellness: how ageing Australians experience health information literacy, *The Australian Library Journal* (ALJ), **58** (3), 269–85.

Yates, C., Partridge, H. and Bruce, C. S. (2012) Exploring Information Experiences Through Phenomenography, *Library and Information Research,* **36** (112), www.lirgjournal.org.uk/lir/ojs/index.php/lir/article/viewFile/496/552.

Zhang, X., Majid, S. and Foo, S. (2010) Environmental Scanning: an application of information literacy skills at the workplace, *Journal of Information Science,* **36**, 719–32.

Index

academics 17, 57
ACRL *see* Association of College &
    Research Libraries
action to improve, Informed
    Systems 45–6
aims
    DeVIL project (Determining the
    Value of Information Literacy)
    70–1
    Presenting Information
    Intelligence and Knowledge
    (PIIK) 121–2
    this book's 2
assessments, Presenting Information
    Intelligence and Knowledge
    (PIIK) 127
Association of College & Research
    Libraries (ACRL) 17, 27, 101
audit, IL 31

benefits
    IL 4, 5, 11, 68–70
    Informed Systems 44–5
best practice 6, 90–4
    research evidence 93–4
    Workplace Experience

Framework 154, 156–7, 160–1
building blocks, data analysis 19–21

career development
    IL's role 37–9, 118–29
    Presenting Information
    Intelligence and Knowledge
    (PIIK) 118–29
case study
    developing IL 143–5
    DeVIL project (Determining the
    Value of Information Literacy)
    71–9
    value, IL 143–5
    workplace IL experience 71–9,
    143–5
Categories of Description 30
    data analysis 21–6
    investigating workplace IL
    experience 16–17
    nursing experience study 21–5,
    32–3
    personal dimension 30, 31–3
    task-focused knowledge
    development 26
    types 26

categorization, data analysis 18
chaotic zone, workplace IL
    experience 137–9
Chartered Institute of Public
    Relations (CIPR) accreditation,
    Presenting Information
    Intelligence and Knowledge
    (PIIK) 127, 128
CISSP (Certified Information
    Systems Security Professional),
    information competences 73
clients' needs/relations 4, 6, 141
    DeVIL project (Determining the
        Value of Information Literacy)
        75–8, 82
    Dimensions of Variation 19
    Evidence-based Practice 93, 95
    Presenting Information
        Intelligence and Knowledge
        (PIIK) 122–3
    value, IL 73, 75–8
collaborative dimension
    see also teamwork
    IL 34–5, 43–55, 61–3, 68, 74–5, 103,
        105, 111–12, 143, 145–6
collective nature of work, practice-
    based learning design 103
company culture see organizational
    culture
competence see information
    competences; professional
    competence
complexity in IL experience,
    personal dimension 31–3
conceptualizing IL learning design
    107–11
constructivist approach, information
    13–14
contexts, investigating workplace IL
    experience 59–61
contextual dimension, IL 34–5
contextual information, using 13–14

continuous workplace learning,
    Informed Systems 47–8
contrast, Dimension of Variation
    154
culture, organizational see
    organizational culture
current models, IL 100–2

DASIL (Dimensions of Activity and
    Skills of Information Literacy),
    practice-based approach to
    teaching IL 105–7
data analysis 159–63
    building blocks 19–21
    Categories of Description 21–6
    categorization 18
    Dimensions of Variation 19–24,
        159, 161
    interview v. questionnaire 161–3
    investigating workplace IL
        experience 18–21
    nursing experience study 159–61
    transcript sorting/analysing 19
data collection, investigating
    workplace IL experience 17–18
definitions
    IL 17, 25, 68, 140–3
    phenomenography 16
    profession 59–60
    workplace 60
    workplace IL experience 15
Dervin's Sense-Making
    Methodology 139–41
developing IL 7–9, 118–29
    case study 143–5
    intermediate stage 110
    preparatory stages 109–10
    stages 109–11
    transition to the workplace
        110–11
developing information
    professionals (IP) 113–29

DeVIL project (Determining the
    Value of Information Literacy)
    70–83
  aims 70–1
  case study 71–9
  clients' needs/relations 75–8, 82
  findings 71–8
  information systems 75–6
  investment categories 72–8
  organizational culture 72–5
  outreach 78
  practices 76–7
  security 68, 73, 75, 77
  sharing data/information 76–7
  space 77
  staff development 72–5
  staff support and guidance 72–5
  value propositions 79–83
'digital and literate', v. 'digitally
    literate' 114–15
Dimensions of Variation
  clients' needs/relations 19
  contrast 154
  data analysis 19–24, 159, 161
  fusion 155
  generalization 154
  nursing experience study 159–61
  separation 155
  Workplace Experience
    Framework 153–5
discourse communities 15
disguised IL, workplace IL
    experience 135–6

education and training 6, 7, 16, 27,
    30, 33, 38, 61, 94–7, 105–12, 143–5
  evidence-based IL education
    149–64
effectiveness zone, workplace IL
    experience 137–9
efficiency, valuing IL 78–9
efficiency zone, workplace IL

    experience 137–9
electronic resources management
    (ERM)
  Informed Systems 50–1
  University of Colorado Denver
    Library 50–1
elements, Informed Systems 53
embodied nature of work, practice-
    based learning design 104
empowerment, relationships, IL
    33–6, 37
ERM see electronic resources
    management
ethical dimensions, nursing
    experience study 87–90
ethical role, IL 6, 20, 21, 37, 76,
    85–96
evidence-based IL education,
    Workplace Experience
    Framework 149–64
Evidence-based Practice 6
  best practice 93–4
  clients' needs/relations 93, 95
  IL's role 86–96
  research evidence 93–4
examples
  investigating workplace IL
    experience 21–5
  Workplace Experience
    Framework 155–157
experience, workplace IL see
    workplace IL experience
Experience Framework 8

firefighters 34, 57
foundations 116–17
fusion, Dimension of Variation
    155

generalization, Dimension of
    Variation 154

higher education xiii, xiv, 7, 68, 97,
    108–9, 113–29
historical and social antecedents,
    practice-based learning design
    104

IL *see* Information Literacy
implications for the future
    value, IL 145–6
    workplace IL experience 145–6
information and knowledge
    management, Presenting
    Information Intelligence and
    Knowledge (PIIK) 123–5
information and knowledge
    workers 8
information competences
    CISSP (Certified Information
    Systems Security Professional)
    73
    professional qualifications 73
information horizon 55
    personal dimension 30–3, 37–9
information intensification 99–100
information landscapes 15, 49, 68,
    69, 79, 83, 98, 100–3, 111–12, 145
Information Literacy (IL)
    benefits 4, 5, 11, 68–70
    defining 17, 25, 68, 140–3
information professionals (IP)
    see also staff ...; web professionals
    developing 113–29
    roles 7–9
information resilience, workplace
    changes 97–8
information resources: producers
    and users, Presenting
    Information Intelligence and
    Knowledge (PIIK) 125
information services, Presenting
    Information Intelligence and
    Knowledge (PIIK) 126

information systems, DeVIL project
    (Determining the Value of
    Information Literacy) 75–6
information-literate workplace 4–6
information-to-knowledge
    connection 150
Informed Learning 27–8, 41–55
    phenomenography 42–3
    relational approach 42–3
Informed Systems 4–5, 41–55
    action to improve 45–6
    benefits 44–5
    continuous workplace learning
    47–8
    critical features 43–4
    electronic resources management
    (ERM) 50–1
    elements 46–8, 53
    evolution 43–6
    leadership activities 54
    organizational readiness 53–4
    organizational transformation
    48–55
    outcomes 45–6, 48–51
    research 43–6
    theory to practice 44–5
    transferability 52–3
    workplace elements 53
    workplace learning synergies
    48–50
innovation zone, workplace IL
    experience 137–9
interview v. questionnaire, data
    analysis 161–3
intimacy, relationships, IL 37
investigating workplace IL
    experience 15–27, 58–9
    see also workplace IL experience
    Categories of Description 16–17
    contexts 59–61
    data analysis 18–21
    data collection 17–18

investigating workplace IL
experience (*continued0*
example 21–5
methodology 15–17
phenomenography 16–17, 151,
152, 161–2
profession context 59–61
relational approach 4, 17, 58, 59,
61, 150–1
IP *see* information professionals

knowledge, workplace 13
knowledge and information
workers 8

leadership activities, Informed
Systems 54
learning outcomes, Presenting
Information Intelligence and
Knowledge (PIIK) 122–3, 127
lessons learned
value, IL 145–6
workplace IL experience 145–6
librarian-centric view, v. user-
centric view 113–14
librarians' roles, workplace
transition resilience 111–12
literacies of information 102–3

methodology, investigating
workplace IL experience
15–17

new versions of work 99–100
nursing experience study
Categories of Description 21–5,
32–3
data analysis 159–61
Dimensions of Variation 159–61
ethical dimensions 87–90
personal effectiveness 35–6
roles, IL's 87–90

Workplace Experience
Framework 153
workplace IL experience 11–12,
21–5, 32–3, 87–90, 153

operating zones
chaotic zone 137–9
effectiveness zone 137–9
efficiency zone 137–9
innovation zone 137–9
workplace IL experience 137–9
organizational culture
DeVIL project (Determining the
Value of Information Literacy)
72–5
IL requirements 139–40
organizational perspective, IL 14
organizational readiness, Informed
Systems 53–4
organizational transformation
Informed Systems 48–55
University of Colorado Denver
Library 50–1
organizing information in practice,
Presenting Information
Intelligence and Knowledge
(PIIK) 126
outcomes
Informed Systems 45–6, 48–51
learning outcomes, Presenting
Information Intelligence and
Knowledge (PIIK) 122–3, 127
research 30–1
outreach, DeVIL project
(Determining the Value of
Information Literacy) 78

paradigms 99–100, 119
personal development 30, 135
personal dimension
Categories of Description 30, 31–3
complexity in IL experience 31–3

personal dimension (*continued*)
IL 4, 29–39
information horizon 30–3, 37–9
personal effectiveness 35–6
relationships, IL 33–6
research data 30–1
personal effectiveness 35–6
nursing experience study 35–6
Phenomenographic–Variation
Theory 152
phenomenography
defining 16
Informed Learning 42–3
investigating workplace IL
experience 16–17, 151, 152,
161–2
learning approach 42–3
relational approach 41–3
PIIK *see* Presenting Information
Intelligence and Knowledge
practice-based approach to teaching
IL 105–7
DASIL (Dimensions of Activity
and Skills of Information
Literacy) 105–7
practice-based learning design 103–
5
collective nature of work 103
embodied nature of work 104
historical and social antecedents
104
relational nature of work 104
socio-materiality of work 103
transition to the workplace 104–5
Presenting Information Intelligence
and Knowledge (PIIK) 7–8
aims 121–2
assessments 127
career development 118–29
Chartered Institute of Public
Relations (CIPR) accreditation
127, 128

clients' needs/relations 122–3
content 123–8
information and knowledge
management 123–5
information resources: producers
and users 125
information services 126
learning outcomes 122–3, 127
module rationale 119–20
module structure 120–8
organizing information in practice
126
philosophy 119
process 123–128
professional development 118–29
purpose 119
strategy, policy and planning 126
technology and the digital
information economy 125
workplace development 128–9
problem, workplace IL experience
132–4
profession, defining 59–60
profession context
investigating workplace IL
experience 59–61
v. workplace context 59–61
professional competence, IL's role 6,
7–8, 25–6, 38, 68–9, 89–96, 118–29
professional development
IL's role 37–9, 118–29
Presenting Information
Intelligence and Knowledge
(PIIK) 118–29
professional qualifications
CISSP (Certified Information
Systems Security Professional)
73
information competences 73
profitability, valuing IL 78–9
progress assessment, IL education 8,
157–9

promoting IL 2, 7–9

questionnaire v. interview, data
     analysis 161–3

real-world experiences 14–15
reconceptualizing IL 1
relational approach
   Informed Learning 41–3
   investigating workplace IL
      experience 4, 17, 58, 59, 61,
      150–1
   learning approach 41–3, 150–1
   phenomenography 41–3
relational nature of work, practice-
   based learning design 104
relationships, IL
   empowerment 33–6, 37
   teamwork 33–7
research xiii–xiv, 1–6, 8–9, 14–28,
   62–6
   findings 87–90
   Informed Systems 43–6
   methodology 15–25, 158–62
   outcomes 30–1
   workplace IL research 98–9, 101
research evidence
   best practice 93–4
   Evidence-based Practice 93–4
returns on investment in IL 78–79
roles
   information professionals (IP)
      7–9
   librarians' 111–12
   workplace transition resilience
      111–12
roles, IL's
   awareness 86
   career development 37–9, 118–29
   communities' role 101
   ethical role 6, 20, 21, 37, 76,
      85–96

Evidence-based Practice 86–96
   nursing experience study 87–90
   professional competence 6, 7–8,
      25–6, 38, 68–9, 89–96, 118–29
   professional development 37–9,
      118–29
   role studies 2

security, DeVIL project
   (Determining the Value of
   Information Literacy) 68, 73, 75,
   77
separation, Dimension of Variation
   155
sharing data/information, DeVIL
   project (Determining the Value
   of Information Literacy) 76–7
skills, workplace 13
sociological–contextual–
   collaborative dimension of
   focus, IL 34–5
socio-materiality of work, practice-
   based learning design 103
space, DeVIL project (Determining
   the Value of Information
   Literacy) 77
'spatial map' 115–6
staff development
   see also information professionals
   (IP)
   DeVIL project (Determining the
   Value of Information Literacy)
   72–5
staff support and guidance, DeVIL
   project (Determining the Value
   of Information Literacy) 72–5
staff turnover, valuing IL 79
strategy, policy and planning,
   Presenting Information
   Intelligence and Knowledge
   (PIIK) 126

task-focused knowledge
development
Categories of Description 26
IL as 25–7
teaching IL
see also practice-based learning
design
conceptualizing IL learning
design 107–11
DASIL (Dimensions of Activity
and Skills of Information
Literacy) 105–7
practice-based approach 105–7
teamwork 14, 19, 23, 27–8
see also collaborative dimension
relationships, IL 33–7
technology and the digital
information economy,
Presenting Information
Intelligence and Knowledge
(PIIK) 125
theory to practice, Informed
Systems 44–5
training see education and training
transcript sorting/analysing, data
analysis 19
transferability, Informed Systems
52–3
transferable skills 114–15
transition to the workplace xiii, xiv,
98–102, 106–9, 149–50
developing IL 110–11
practice-based learning design
104–5
resilience 111–12
trust, relationships, IL 37

University of Colorado Denver
Library
electronic resources management
(ERM) 50–1
organizational transformation 50–1

user-centric view, v. librarian-
centric view 113–14

value, IL 5–6, 12–15, 67–83, 131–47
approach 70–1
case study 143–5
clients' needs/relations 73, 75–8
DeVIL project (Determining the
Value of Information Literacy)
70–83
efficiency 78–9
implications for the future 145–6
lessons learned 145–6
profitability 78–9
returns on investment in IL 78–9
staff turnover 79
Variation Theory of learning 8, 66,
150, 152, 153
Virtuality 5, 57–66
contexts, workplace IL experience
59–61
enabler of professional IL 63–4
Virtual workplace v. Virtuality at
work 62–4
web professionals 57–66

ways of thinking about IL 12–15
contextual information, using
13–14
organizational perspective 14
real-world experiences 14–15
skills and knowledge in the
workplace 13
web professionals 1–3, 8, 27, 58, 68,
94
see also information professionals
(IP)
experience, workplace IL 57–66
Virtuality 57–66
workplace, defining 60
workplace changes, information
resilience 97–8

workplace context, v. profession
context 59–61
workplace development
IL 128–9
markers 129
Presenting Information
Intelligence and Knowledge
(PIIK) 128–9
workplace elements, Informed
Systems 53
Workplace Experience Framework
149–64
best practice 154, 156–7, 160–1
Dimensions of Variation 153–5
evidence-based IL education
149–64
example 155–7
nursing study 153
workplace IL experience 3
see also investigating workplace IL
experience
case study 71–9, 143–5
defining 15
discovering the details 151

disguised IL 135–6
IL concept 141–3
IL requirements, organizational
culture 139–40
implications for the future 145–6
information intensification 99–100
lessons learned 145–6
monitoring students 158–9
new versions of work 99–100
nursing study 11–12, 21–5, 32–3,
87–90, 153
operating zones 137–9
problem 132–4
ranges of experiences 158
recognizing IL 135–7
redefining IL 140–3
web professionals 57–66
workplace IL research 98–9, 101
workplace learning synergies,
Informed Systems 48–50

Yammer, enterprise social network
73, 74, 75